In this honest, remarkable memoir, Earl Hamner writes of the many generous women who have influenced his life. "Some of these ladies have been famous," he writes, "their names and faces known all over the world. Others are known only in their own communities. But their gifts have been many and varied, and each has enriched my life."

First there was Doris Giannini Hamner, the gentle woman who gave him the gift of life. Other Hamner women were also generous with him. Foremost is his wife, Jane Martin Hamner, who has given him the gift of love. In his teenage years, his father's three sisters—Nora, Margaret, and Lottie—provided him a home in town so he could attend college. Later, his daughter, Caroline, gave him the gift of love—again.

Women of Schuyler, Virginia, where he grew up, also gave generous- to the eldest Hamner son. Parkie Sneed, a neighbor, gave him his first job when he was ten. Sixth-grade teacher Mrs. Olive Giannini inspired him with a memorable quotation in his "autograph book." Elsie Mayo Gusmerotti, another teacher, awakened his first stirrings of puppy love. And Aunt Myrle Timberlake paid him a quarter for a summer's work, giving him the gift of "big money."

Many others have given generously too: magazine editor Minda Barton; Dorothy McCann, who gave him his first "big-time" writing job at NBC; Mabel Wheaton, the sister of Thomas Wolfe; writers Harper Lee and Kay Thompson; editor Belle Becker of Random House; First Lady Eleanor Roosevelt; actresses Tallulah Bankhead, Patricia Neal, Michael Learned, Jane Wyman, and Ellen Corby; entertainer Minnie Pearl; presidential mother Lillian Carter—so many!

Generous Women is a warm thank-you to the women who have shaped the author into the man he has become. Indeed, this fond appreciation is a reminder that all of us are nurtured, enriched, and sustained by the generous gifts of others.

Early Praise for *Generous Women*

"Earl Hamner has written a rare and beautiful memoir in the form of a thank-you note to all the women in his life who helped him along the way. Wonderful and touching portraits of fascinating and interesting women from Harper Lee to Tallulah Bankhead. Charming and highly readable. I couldn't put it down."

— Fannie Flagg, author of *Fried Green Tomatoes at the Whistle Stop Cafe, Can't Wait to Get to Heaven*, and many other bestsellers

"Men, read this book if you want to know how to dazzle women. Girls, Mr. Hamner is a man who knows how to treat a lady!"

— Rita Mae Brown, best-selling author of *Sour Puss* and other Mrs. Murphy mysteries

"Somehow Earl Hamner has led a fuller life than anybody else I've ever heard of — or maybe he's just got the quickest eye, the keenest ear, the truest voice, and the best memory in the world. Surely, he's got the biggest heart! And his thoughtfulness . . . here, he thanks the women who have given him 'gifts' throughout his life, from his mother and beloved neighbors, teachers, and aunts to such unexpected influences as Tallulah Bankhead, Harper Lee, and Minnie Pearl. What he doesn't tell is how much his friendship must have meant to each of them. These lovely portraits of influential women in Earl Hamner's life combine to create an unusual autobiography of a most generous man."

— Lee Smith, author of *The Last Girls* and *On Agate Hill*

Generous Women
An Appreciation

EARL HAMNER

CUMBERLAND HOUSE
NASHVILLE, TENNESSEE

GENEROUS WOMEN
Published by Cumberland House Publishing, Inc.
431 Harding Industrial Drive
Nashville, TN 37211

Cover design: Unlikely Suburban Design
Text design: Lisa Taylor

Library of Congress Cataloging-in-Publication Data

Hamner, Earl.
  Generous women : an appreciation / Earl Hamner.
    p. cm.
  ISBN-13: 978-1-684-42495-5 (pbk)
  ISBN-13: 978-1-58182-553-4 (hc)
  ISBN-10: 1-58182-553-6
  1. Hamner, Earl—Friends and associates. 2. Hamner, Earl—Family.
3. Authors, American—20th century—Biography. 4. Television producers and directors—United States—Biography. 5. Women—United States—Biography. I. Title.

PS3558.A456Z46 2006
813'.54—dc22

                                                    2006025171

3 4 5 6 7 — 11 10 09 08 07

Dedication

With this book I wish to salute, thank, and celebrate the lives of some ladies who have shaped me into the man I have become. I am grateful to each of them, but I especially want to express my love and gratitude to my wife, Jane, who has enriched my life most of all, and to whom these pages are dedicated.

CONTENTS

INTRODUCTION 13

THE GIFT OF LIFE 17
Doris Giannini Hamner — Mother

THE GIFT OF EMPLOYMENT 29
Parkie Sneed — Neighbor

THE GIFT OF INSPIRATION 35
Olive Giannini — Teacher

THE GIFT OF PUPPY LOVE 39
Elsie Mayo Gusmerotti — Teacher

THE GIFT OF BIG MONEY 43
Myrle Timberlake — Aunt

THE GIFT OF EDUCATION 53
Nora Spencer Hamner — Aunt
Margaret Hamner Myers — Aunt
Lottie Hamner Dover — Aunt

THE GIFT OF A LANDMARK 67
Jeanine — Friend

Contents

The Gift of Encouragement 83
Mina Barton — Editor

The Gift of Paradise 87
B. B. Caverly — Landlady

The Gift of the Big Time 95
Dorothy McCann — Producer

The Gift of Love 103
Jane Martin Hamner — Wife

The Gift of the Big Easy 113
Frances Parkinson Keyes — Novelist

The Gift of Literature 121
Mabel Wheaton — Thomas Wolfe's Sister

The Gift of Achievement 129
Belle Becker — Random House Editor

The Gift of Validation 139
Harper Lee — Novelist

The Gift of Patience 145
Eleanor Roosevelt — Herself

The Gift of Fun 149
Tallulah Bankhead — Actress

THE GIFT OF KINDNESS 159
Kay Thompson — Personality

THE GIFT OF STYLE 163
Patricia Neal — Actress

THE GIFT OF UNDERSTANDING 169
Michael Learned — Actress

THE GIFT OF COURAGE 181
Ellen Corby — Actress

THE GIFT OF CONCERN 189
Lillian Carter — Herself

THE GIFT OF GRACIOUSNESS 193
Minnie Pearl — Personality

THE GIFT OF ROYALTY 199
Jane Wyman — Actress

THE GIFT OF SOLACE 205
Isis Ringrose — Friend

THE GIFT OF LANGUAGE 221
Agripina Salvador — Friend

THE GIFT OF LOVE (AGAIN) 229
Caroline Spencer Hamner — Daughter

Generous Women

INTRODUCTION

One of my favorite books is Thomas Wolfe's autobiographical novel, *Look Homeward, Angel*. It is a very personal book to me because it tells the story of a boy from the Southern mountains who leaves home to realize his passion to become a writer, but in all of his journeys he returns home, to the place and people he left behind, for his inspiration and his strength. I have reread the book from time to time, and not long ago I came across this sentence: "But we are the sum of all the moments of our lives—all that is ours is in them: we cannot escape or conceal it." And it prompted me to count some of the influences on my life and how they led me to become the man I am today.

Each of our lives is the result of a myriad of encounters with an astonishing variety of our fellow human beings. Each of our days is comprised of endless events, some of such little import that we forget them immediately. Others are of monumental sadness or cause for elation. Much of the time we can choose these events by selecting where we want to be at a given moment or the company we keep, an ambition, a failure or victory, some path we take; but just as often as not we are exposed to events over which we have no control.

When these events are of little importance they make only a passing impression on our lives. The result is temporary, quickly forgotten, as we go on to the next encounter of our day. A frown from a friend or loved one can evoke a temporary feeling of sadness or rejection—a cloud that passes until the dark day turns sunny again. A smile can cause a joyful or pleasurable response that leaves a warm spot in the heart until it is erased by the next event that enters our consciousness.

The greater influences on our lives are felt when a person does something that has a permanent effect on us that changes our lives for better or for worse. For the most part, most of our daily encounters are positive and pleasant. We receive love from family members and are stronger for it. We feel fondness from friends and life feels good. Coworkers can make the job more pleasant with an offer to help or affectionate banter and the day is shorter and the workload is lighter.

I began reflecting on Thomas Wolfe's theory and looking back on the "sums I had not counted," especially on the truly meaningful and positive events that shaped my life. For the most part, these occasions have been with women, generous women. Some of these ladies have been famous, their names and faces known all over the world. Others are known only in their own communities, but their gifts have been many and varied, and each has enriched my life.

So here's a salute, a thank you, and a celebration of some ladies who vary from a former first lady of our country to a notorious Broadway actress, from my mother to my daughter, from a mystic to a house-keeper. I am grateful to each of them, but I especially want to express my love and gratitude to my wife, Jane, who has enriched my life most of all.

THE GIFT OF LIFE

Doris Giannini Hamner—Mother

This is a book about women who have given me gifts, who have enriched my life and who have contributed to my becoming the man I am today. It seems only right and proper that the name of Doris Giannini Hamner be given special recognition, for it was she who gave me the gift of life.

I was born in the early morning on the tenth of July, 1923, in the Daniel J. Carroll Memorial Hospital in Schuyler, Virginia, a small community in the Blue Ridge about twenty-five miles south of Charlottesville. The delivery was made by Dr. Alexander Augustus Sizer, assisted by his wife and nurse, Jeanette Brooks Sizer.

It was an interesting time to enter the world. A Frenchman named Emile Coue came to America spreading his philosophy of determining our destiny by auto-suggestion. "Day by day, in every way, I'm getting better and better" was his mantra. But the omens for the world were not quite so optimistic.

Doris Giannini Hamner

Adolf Hitler held a meeting in Munich where the swastika first appeared as a symbol of the Nazi Party. A doctor in Paris proclaimed smoking beneficial to one's health. The Imperial Wizard announced that the KKK had a membership of more than a million men. Sarah Bernhardt died, and Bessie Smith summed it all up with her song "Downhearted Blues."

In spite of the grim news of the day my arrival seems to have been greeted with joy by my parents and was the beginning of a peace treaty between my Grandmother Ora and my father.

My mother's mother, Miss Ora Lee Giannini, was Baptist. And she was Baptist to an alarming degree. She disapproved of dancing, swearing, card playing, hand holding, overly long kisses, any public display of affection, and raised voices on Sunday. She used the word *honey-fuggen* to describe hugging, kissing, touching, glancing affectionately at another person, suggestive behavior of any kind and, presumably, sexual intercourse. I thought the word was her own invention and used it in my novel *Fifty Roads to Town*. Bennett Cerf, then president of Random House, was delighted with the word and claimed he would someday include it in the *Random House Dictionary*. If he did, I have never been able to find it there. Perhaps someone on his editorial staff might have found it too risqué.

The last person in the world my grandmother would have selected as a suitor for her sixteen-year-old daughter was my father. He was twenty at the time, a known carouser, a gambler, a drinker, a dancer, a crack shot, and—benefiting his Welsh ancestry—he was a singer of note. He thought nothing of going hunting on Sunday. An even more despicable crime was when he defiled Sunday by going fishing. To get to the Rockfish River he had to go right past the

Baptist church. In the church they would be singing "Shall We Gather at the River?" and going past he would smile and nod in complete agreement.

My grandmother forbade my mother to see my father but somehow they managed to have a courtship. My father proposed. My mother accepted, and they slipped away to the county seat at Lovingston to obtain the license. That night when she was supposed to be at Wednesday Night Prayer Meeting my mother met my father. They went to the Baptist Parsonage to ask Preacher Hicks to marry them. Preacher Hicks had a mild stutter, which became intense when he was under stress. He was now under stress. He knew that my grandmother would have a tizzy-fit if he married her daughter to a man she disapproved of without limits. When my father handed him the license, Preacher Hicks, according to my father's account, said, "I cannot marry you!"

My mother used to tell how at that point she became frightened and asked my father to take her home.

Instead my father said to the preacher, "You're not the only damn preacher in the county. We'll find us another one!"

Preacher Hicks replied, stuttering badly, "Under the c-c-c-c-circumstances, I will marry you," and he did.

Neighbors predicted that the marriage would not last six months. Her mother swore never to speak to her daughter again, but in time Miss Ora came around and gradually she saw that her daughter had tamed her young man. He mended his ways, got himself baptized, joined the church, and said goodbye to his fast friends. They had forty-five good years together, and to his dying day he called our mother "Sweetheart."

My mother and father had a good marriage. They genuinely loved and respected each other. Some evidence that they got along reasonably well is that eight children were the result of their love. Cliff was the next child after me. Then came the first girl, Marion, followed by another daughter, Audrey. Paul was next, then Bill, then Jim, and then the baby, Nancy Alice. Three of my brothers are dead: Cliff, Bill, and Jim. Paul is my only remaining brother. At Thanksgiving of 2004 we lost my sister Marion, so there are two sisters left.

I once wrote: "We see each other when we can. We drink 'the recipe' and gather around the piano with our arms around each other and sing the old songs we grew up with like 'The Old Rugged Cross' and 'Let Me Call You Sweetheart.' Needless to say when we come together for our family gatherings we do not sing so zestfully as we once did, and our reunions are not as joyful as they once were."

A formidable event shadowed the early years of our parents' life together: the Great Depression. It made them frugal, and more often than not they passed that quality down to their children.

It called upon them to be resourceful and inventive. My mother was a quilter, and even when I had grown up, on visiting home, to sleep covered with one of my mother's quilts brought special warmth. She made many of my sisters' dresses on her Singer sewing machine from patterns ordered from McCall's or Good Housekeeping. Clothing was handed down from the oldest to the youngest. Sometimes a boy's shirt landed on one of the girls or the pants didn't fit the younger brother, and if we complained my mother would say, "They're clean and you'll wear them."

The Depression called upon our parents also to use traditional means of survival. All the families in Schuyler kept pigs and there was always a cow out grazing somewhere. Each family had a garden, and during the summer our mother would "put up" vegetables and berries and fruit. I can still remember the wonderful vinegary aroma that permeated the house after the first frost when my mother pickled the last of the tomatoes and made green tomato relish. And the sausage she and my grandmother made when we slaughtered hogs after the first frost was so pungent and peppery, it makes me hungry just to think of it.

While our mother did the canning, our father shot quail and pheasant, venison, squirrel, and rabbit. He brought black bass and catfish caught from the Rock-

fish River and at Thanksgiving there was never a
store-bought turkey, but one that came from the
neighboring hills and woods. We knew it came from
that flock over on Wales Mountain because we had
watched the flock nest and thrive for generations.
Usually it still had birdshot in it.

Last Thanksgiving my wife and children and I had
our Thanksgiving dinner at a restaurant in New York
that had received extremely high ratings from the
food critics. The turkey was excellent even though
there was not a single pellet of birdshot in it.

When we were growing up, each night my mother
helped us with our homework. We all sat on benches
around the long wooden kitchen table that my father
had built.

The youngest child was helped first, and then
shooed off to bed. And then the next-oldest child's
arithmetic or geography problem was solved and
checked.

My mother had a beautiful singing voice. I once
said, "She sang her way through the Depression." She
loved the sentimental tunes like "I'll Take You Home
Again, Kathleen" or "When You and I Were Young,
Maggie." I can still hear her singing one of her favorites, "Ramona":

Ramona, when day is done I hear your call,
Ramona, we'll meet beside the waterfall.

I dread the dawn
When I awake to find you gone,
Ramona, I love you, my own.

After I moved to New York and was working at NBC, I persuaded my mother to come and visit. When she arrived I asked her if there was anything special she would like to do. Without hesitation she said, "I would like to see Arthur!"

Arthur was Arthur Godfrey, a radio talk show host of the day, a folksy, down-home guy that my mother adored. She told me that he had said on the air that he frequently went to "The Hawaiian Room" in the Lexington Hotel, so I made reservations.

The Hawaiian Room was kind of sweet and corny, with a band playing Hawaiian music and girls doing the hula in grass skirts. While we waited for Arthur to make an appearance I played a dirty trick on my mother. If she hated anything in the world it was alcohol. When the waiter came I ordered her a mai-tai, thinking she might like it because the sweet taste would disguise the rum flavor. The mai-tai arrived, a beautiful creation with a small purple Japanese umbrella for decoration. She took one taste, looked at me and said, "This thing has alcohol in it!" She pushed it away and I ordered her lemonade. We went to the Hawaiian Room twice, but Arthur never showed up.

Where she ever found the time to read I cannot

imagine, but somehow she did. She loved to read the *Bible*, and accepted every word of it as the gospel truth. One of her favorite books was called *Heart-throbs*, a collection of poems and essays that she loved.

Her favorite book of all was *A Lantern in Her Hand* by Bess Streeter Aldrich. It is the story of a woman who has artistic talent and ambitions, but weighed down by the necessity of caring for her family, she never achieves them herself. As the years pass she comes to realize that each of her children has found success in those professions she yearned for, and it is a rewarding and moving realization for her.

A television producer once approached me and asked if there was some project I loved that I would like to write. I said I had one project that I had never entrusted to anyone because it had to be done with love and respect by all concerned since it would be a tribute to my mother. I suggested *A Lantern in Her Hand*. And my writing partner at the time, Don Sipes, and I adapted the book for television. The closing narration is about the main character in the book, but it might just as well be about my mother:

> My mother lived into her eighties. She remained in the house she and my father had built where she had raised her family.
>
> Watching her children and her

grandchildren she realized all of her
dreams and she continued to enrich our
lives as well.

When my television series *The Waltons* became a
success in the early 1970s, fans began showing up in
Schuyler and stopping to see my mother. My father
had died in 1969 and I think she had grown lonely and
welcomed the callers.

She would invite total strangers in for tea and in
time her tea bills became exorbitant. Occasionally I
would call home and she would say, "There's the
nicest young couple here from Ireland." Or "A woman
came by today and asked me for my autograph. Lord
knows what good it will do her!" Or "I've made
friends with a family from Germany. They say I make
the best biscuits they ever tasted!"

Over the years she inspired many of the characters
I wrote about. In the movie *Spencer's Mountain*, her
character was portrayed by Maureen O'Hara. In my
CBS Playhouse "Appalachian Autumn," the role was
played by Teresa Wright. Elizabeth Huddle portrayed
her in my series *Boone*. Patricia Neal gave a strong and
unforgettable touch to the role of Olivia in *The Homecoming*, as did Michael Learned when she brought her
own special gifts to the character in *The Waltons*.

In time my mother would visit us in California.
One of her favorites things to do was to visit Stage 26

at Warner Brothers Studio where *The Waltons* was being filmed. We had a large number of children in the cast. When child actors are being filmed the law requires that a parent or guardian be present. Therefore, there were a number of mothers sitting on the side of the set knitting, reading, or watching. My mother enjoyed joining the group and watching the scenes being filmed.

The first time she came to see us in California she flew from Virginia alone. It was her first flight and I worried about her. I was waiting at LAX when her flight arrived. Passengers began streaming out of the arrival gate. Many of them were shaken and I overheard remarks such as: "I will never get on another airplane as long as I live." "It was the worst flight I have ever experienced." "I thought that turbulence was going to break the damn plane in half."

I did not see any sign of my mother. I was very concerned. More passengers emerged, all of them complaining about the bad flight.

Finally I spotted her. She walked jauntily toward me, smiling happily, and completely at ease.

"How was your flight?" I asked.

"It was a little bumpy, but I enjoyed it," she said. "But I don't think some of the others did. Maybe it was their first flight."

During the last fifteen years of her life she was afflicted with Alzheimer's. It came on so gradually that at first we did not recognize it for what it was. She became forgetful, could not remember names, and would order forty-five pounds of ground round at the market or would be despondent, which was not her true nature. As time went by, she was presented each day with new symptoms of the disease. She became more and more difficult to take care of. My brother Jim took on the responsibility of her care. A nurse stayed with her during the day and Jim would take care of her after he came home from work in the evening.

"I want to go home," she would cry.

No amount of assurance that she was already at home would comfort her. Sometimes we would coax her into the car and drive around for a while hoping it would comfort her, and sometimes it did.

At other times she would slip away and someone would have to go find her, always looking for "home." I have decided that "home" was not a place, but a time—a time when we children were still young, when my father was alive, and when she was happy.

The last time I saw her she asked, "Who are you?"

I said, "I'm Earl. I'm your son."

"Where do you live?" she asked.

"In California," I told her.

"That's so interesting," she said. "I have a son in California."

It broke my heart.

THE GIFT OF EMPLOYMENT
Parkie Sneed—Neighbor

I have never measured success in terms of income or possessions. Success to me seems made up of a lot of things. Can I go to sleep peacefully at night knowing I have used the day to its fullest potential? Can I look my friends and family in the eye with a clear conscience? Can I look myself in the eye in the mirror? Have I inadvertently wounded any person during the day? If I have touched anyone's life, did I in some small way make his or her life better?

Some people have seen my "success" in a different way. They consider me successful because in their eyes I have made a lot of money, or because on a modest scale my name is known, or simply because my career has led me from the backwoods of Virginia to Hollywood, California.

I have known a few people in the industry who claim to have helped me along the road to "success" by giving me my first job. I thank each and every one of you, but you did not give me my first job!

In truth, my first job came about when I was ten years old. Living across the road from us in a square white house was a neighbor named Parkie Sneed. Mrs. Sneed lived all alone. There had been a son named Claudie who died of tuberculosis and a daughter who lived in Detroit. Her daughter would visit her mother from time to time but mostly Miss Parkie's days and hours were solitary ones. She appreciated music, and had a Victrola as well as a piano. Both the piano and the Victrola were part of the furnishings in the "parlor," which was located to the right of the front door off of the main hall and separated by portieres. The other furniture was made up of a matching sofa and chairs covered in black leather that appeared even darker because the window shades were drawn most of the time to keep the furniture from becoming damaged by the sun.

The house was surrounded by a series of flowerbeds, which Miss Parkie called her garden. It may have been a garden at one time but as the years passed it became an overgrown thicket.

One day she beckoned to me, and when I crossed over to her garden she said, "How would you like to work for me?"

I said that would be fine.

"I'll pay you a dime," she said.

I agreed to work for those wages and took up my first paying job. The job consisted of weeding the overgrown flowerbeds, thinning out bulbs that had multiplied over the years until they were crowded into thick masses, removing dead plants, and transplanting others.

She was a demanding employer, but not an unreasonable one. She stood over me every minute and said things like, "Mind that iris. I set it out the first year we were married."

I learned to have her point out which were weeds and which were flowers because when I inadvertently yanked out what looked like a weed to me it turned out to be an aster. Miss Parkie was not pleased. Sometimes she would stop supervising my gardening and look off into space and sing a little song. One of them went:

> Spring time is coming
> Sweet Fern! Sweet Fern!
> Spring time is coming,
> Sweet Fern.

After we had worked for a while and the day had grown warm she said she thought we both had earned a little lemonade.

We drank our lemonade in the kitchen, and hoping to actually get to see her fabulous music machine, I would ask, "How's your Victrola?"

She said it was just fine and—as I had hoped she

might—she offered to let me see it. Once in the parlor, she wound the Victrola and put on a record. It was Al Jolson singing "Swanee."

> Swanee, how I love ya,
> How I love ya,
> My dear old Swanee
> I'd give the world to be
> Among the folks in D-I-X-I-E!

Miss Parkie joined in, and when I learned the words I sang right along with her. We were having a grand time until she decided it was time to return to my job in the garden.

I continued to work for Miss Parkie all of that summer. I think more than my gardening she valued me for news of what was happening in the community. I was a walking newspaper, since I had a buttermilk route that took me into the kitchens of a good many housewives. This being before we had telephones, it was not unusual for one lady to ask me to pass on a piece of news to the next customer I was delivering to.

Pregnancies, illness, bits of gossip, indiscretions that could be entrusted to a ten-year-old boy all came into my possession. I was a walking custodian of the history of our town, a veritable storehouse of material for a fledgling writer.

As the years passed, Parkie grew a bit erratic. She

seemed not to sleep at night, and we would hear her well past midnight walking through her house and singing. One of the songs she would sing was eerie and haunting:

When my dreamboat comes home
Then I never more will roam
We'll be sweethearts forever
When my dreamboat comes home.

Neighbors were treasures back then and Miss Parkie had been invited to some of our family functions in the past, so when several family members organized a Hamner reunion at Lake Sherando over in the Shenandoah Valley she was included.

At the last minute there was not room for me in any of the family vehicles, so I volunteered to ride with Miss Parkie in her old Model T with the rumble seat. I think my mother was uneasy about the idea but I insisted and she reluctantly allowed me to go.

As she drove along, Miss Parkie sang one song after another in a pretty soprano voice. I joined in if I knew the words. We were singing "You Are My Sunshine" when we started up Afton Mountain, and I realized from the rhythmic, sudden surges in the acceleration of the car that she was keeping time with her foot on the gas pedal.

In her later years, as her health declined, occasionally she would walk around her house in the middle of the night, become disoriented, and call for someone to come and find her. My mother and father would go over and help her into bed.

Miss Parkie had a stroke on the day my sister Marion was married, and she died a short while later. I always remember the lonely old lady who loved music and who gave me my first job.

To this day I cannot drive up Afton Mountain without thinking back to that ride with Parkie Sneed, and once or twice, to the bemusement of the drivers behind me, I have even pumped the accelerator to the tune of "You Are My Sunshine."

THE GIFT OF INSPIRATION

Olive Giannini—Teacher

I have been told that all a person needs is one inspired teacher to turn his or her life in a positive direction. Mrs. Olive Giannini did that for me in a way that even today influences my life and my work. She was a great aunt as well as my sixth-grade teacher.

Back there in a little company town we were in the grip of the Great Depression and the future of the country looked grim. Nor did the future seem to hold much promise for a grade-school, backwoods boy who was bright but who seemed destined for a job in the local soapstone quarry or general store.

In those days school children kept "Autograph Books" in which fellow students would write messages of friendship, declarations of love, or words of encouragement. Often these messages were trite, no matter how lofty the writer's intentions happened to be. But the message could also be inspiring, and that is how it was with what Mrs. Giannini wrote:

Heights of great men reached and kept
Were not attained in sudden flight
But they while their companions slept
Were toiling upward in the night.
— Henry Wadsworth Longfellow

After I graduated I won a scholarship to the University of Richmond. It took care of my tuition, but there were still challenging fees to be paid—food, clothing, streetcar fare, books, lunch—all those items that most young people today take for granted. I had to earn them by finding an extra full-time job after I had attended classes during the day.

Mrs. Giannini's quote helped sustain me while I spent long hours at the Brooks Transportation Company down on the Boulevard, when I forced myself to overcome my fatigue so I could type the bills of lading it was my job to prepare. Later, at midnight when the work was done, I stood in rain or snow on a corner of Broad Street waiting for the streetcar to carry me home. For once the aroma of baking bread was not comforting because the streetcar stop was directly in front of a bakery, and the fact that I was alone and wet and hungry and far from the comforts that baking break usually brought. I would recite the words to the poem and it was sustaining.

Years later, after my career was under way and I was working as a radio writer, I still aspired to write books. And I did not attain my position as a novelist

Olive Giannini

"in sudden flight." I wrote my first two books by writing after a full and demanding day's work at NBC.

But that one schoolteacher's thoughtful words did
more than inspire me. Today that room where Mrs.
Giannini taught sixth grade is visited by thousands of
people from all over the world. It came about in an interesting way.

Some years ago the county closed the school in an economy move. Following the closure of the school the children from my hometown were bussed to a consolidated school at the county seat. For a long time the old school building stood empty. A resourceful county supervisor, Woody Greenberg, put his mind to ways in which the empty building might be put to use. Woody came up with the idea of turning the empty building into the Walton Museum.* Permission to use the school was granted by the county. I persuaded Warner Brothers, who owned the television series, to give their consent. Local people under the guidance of a Schuyler native, Robert Brent Hall, recreated with amazing fidelity rooms that were replicas of the Walton sets as seen on television.

On opening day of the museum some six thousand people found their way to Schuyler, which is difficult to find under any circumstances. There were traffic jams and good-natured crowds milling around the normally sleepy little village. And today they still come from every state in the union as well as from overseas.

And none of them is aware that in the room where the Walton kitchen has been recreated a schoolteacher once wrote an inspired quote in the Autograph Book of one of her students.

---

*Unfortunately, because of an injury done to a member of my family, I no longer support the museum and am in no way associated with it.

THE GIFT OF PUPPY LOVE

Elsie Mayo Gusmerotti—Teacher

I graduated from Schuyler High School in 1940. It was an interesting time in the world. The Great Depression was fairly well over, World War II was brewing, and I was about to leave that warm and secure Hamner nest. I was uncertain of a good many things, but the one thing I knew for sure was that I was in love with Miss Elsie Mayo.

I do not remember what grade she taught. I know she coached the girls' basketball team. Her flowing blonde hair moved in a constantly changing pattern of beauty as she ran alongside the members of the team calling out encouragement or direction. I would make it my business to be a spectator of that sport whenever possible.

To my distress I became aware that she was dating the new math teacher who was also the boys' gym instructor, T. Dan Gusmerotti. I hated his name and I hated his looks. He was dark and handsome, an assured-looking man, very Latin looking.

Elsie Mayo Gusmerotti

Once I became aware of the relationship, I fantasized about how to get rid of him without having to go to jail. As fevered as I was I knew that murdering him robbed me of even the pathetic relationship I had with Miss Mayo, which consisted entirely of worshiping her from afar, calling out "Good morning" and hoping that my squeaky voice would magically shift into bass at least for that moment. Sometimes it would and I imagined that she gazed after me, thinking what an attractive young man I was, and how she might secretly want to get to know me better.

I will never forget the time when I finally achieved the unimaginable: I got to dance with Miss Elsie!

It was a graduation dance. I had slicked down most of my unruly hair, practiced how to make my voice reach the deeper registers, and practiced the "one-step" during the very few minutes when my brothers left me alone in the bedroom where I might have privacy.

The dance was in the auditorium of the school, and most of the dancers were students. Miss Mayo was one of the chaperones, and spent most of her time on the sidelines, but from time to time Mr. T. Dan Gusmerotti, who was also a chaperone, would make his way over to her and lead her out onto the dance floor.

Gathering every ounce of my courage, I found myself "breaking in" and tapping T. Dan Gusmerotti on the shoulder. He stepped aside graciously, and suddenly I held Miss Elsie Mayo in my arms!

It was ecstasy. That voluptuous blonde hair touched my cheek, and I breathed an aroma of spice and citrus. My feet behaved, my voice did not squeal and to my astonishment I began to croon. The song we were dancing to was "Careless."

Careless, now that you've got me loving you.
You're careless, careless in everything you do.
Are you as careless as you seem to be?
Or are you just careless with me?

Miss Mayo seemed unaware of the depth of my passion. Her eyes kept wandering to where Mr. Gusmerotti was watching from the sideline. I resolved right then to murder him at the very first opportunity. What was twenty years in jail compared to the love of a good woman!

I am sure she had no idea how heartbroken I was when at the end of the school year she married T. Dan Gusmerotti.

Over the years I got over my infatuation with Miss Mayo. I left home for college, then went to war, and then began building a career in New York. I had not even thought of her in years until one day I received a letter from one of her nieces telling me that Miss Elsie Mayo Gusmerotti was still alive. She had retired from teaching many years ago, Mr. Gusmerotti had died after a lifetime together, and Miss Elsie was living in a retirement home in Waynesboro, Virginia.

I called the lady. She remembered me as a "good student!" I finally confessed how much I had adored her and as we chatted the whisper of hair against my cheek, the scent of citrus, and words of an old song came stealing back and stabbed my heart.

THE GIFT OF BIG MONEY

Myrle Timberlake—Aunt

I remember the summer my Aunt Myrle was making
big money and paid me a quarter.

Myrle was a younger sister of my mother's. She
lived with us for a while. I can't remember the reason,
but I suspect she volunteered to help my mother cope
with the population explosion that was taking place
in our home. The children ranged in age from an in-
fant up to me, a twelve-year-old. As my father used to
say, "I don't know where they come from, but one
turns up about every nine months and fifteen minutes."

Even though our house was crowded and filled
with the activity of a boisterous family, I suspect that
Myrle was happy to have some respite from the strict
Baptist home her mother kept. There, just about every
activity from kissing to touching between the sexes
was considered sinful. Yet, Miss Ora, as we called my
maternal grandmother, was heard in later life to say:
"There's no difference between the old generation and

this new one. Y'all do in the front porch what we used to do out back!"

I was twelve when Myrle came to live with us. She was a jolly girl and had a keen ability to enjoy life. She had a beautiful shade of red hair and a broad pretty face that came to a ready smile. She had a deeply felt sense of wonder and an appreciation of a variety of life's little pleasures. She would often exclaim, "Don't you just loooove that!" She might be admiring a tree in its autumn colors, a joke, a picture in a magazine, or a song she had heard on the radio. I remember summer evenings, after the supper dishes had been washed and put away, sitting on the porch swing listening to Myrle singing:

When its springtime in the Rockies,
I'll be coming home to you,
Little sweetheart of the mountains,
With your bonny eyes so blue.
Once again, I'll say, "I love you."
While the birds sing all the day
Little sweetheart of the Rockies
Of the Rockies far away.

Those were Depression years, but in our area they were relieved by two financial windfalls. One came in July when peaches became ripe, and the other came in the fall, when the time arrived to harvest apples. A

Myrle Timberlake

crowd of young people would get up before daybreak
and go by truck to the orchards above the town of
Crozet, about fifteen miles away, to join the itinerant
workers when the fruit became ripe.

It was tedious work. The hours were long and the
work was demanding. Heavy baskets of fruit had to
be carefully picked, placed in baskets, and carried

from the trees to the trucks where they were loaded. The pickers would return home after dark. They would have sunburned arms and shreds of leaves in their hair and during peach season they would be covered with peach fuzz.

Each year I was determined that I would join the group, but my parents came up with all sorts of objections. I was too young. I might fall off the ladder and break a bone. You're not old enough! Maybe next year.

Maybe next year was no consolation, and I would get up at four-thirty in the morning and watch with envy as Myrle was helped up into the back of the truck with the other young people who would return home that night weary but rich.

Myrle was exhausted by the end of the day. Afraid that she might oversleep and miss her ride to Crozet, and knowing that I was always up and out watching the morning's exodus, she made a deal with me. I would make certain that she was awake and on time for the departure every day and at the end of the season she would pay me a quarter. That may not sound like much money today, but this was a time when even a good restaurant might serve a steak dinner "with all the trimmings" for forty-seven cents.

When the season was over she paid my salary. I spent hours pondering how to spend it. One of the uses I considered was to buy my way into heaven.

I had been working hard to save my soul that summer. I had learned that "a sin of thought is a sin of deed," and try as I might I could not prevent sins of thought swarming through my head.

My only redemption was to be "born again." I went faithfully to Sunday morning sermons down at the Baptist church, to tent revivals up on the baseball field, to nearby churches of other denominations where exhortations by visiting preachers would work themselves into a frenzy trying to help me receive the Holy Ghost.

I gathered from my research that the signal that one was eligible for salvation would come when God touched the penitent on the shoulder. After that, the sinner would simply go to the mourner's bench, confess his sins, and accept Jesus as his Personal Savior.

I sat on one of those hard Baptist benches, every muscle tense, teeth clenched together, looking over my shoulder in a cold sweat. All the while the congregation was singing in dramatically lowered voices the words I was to use when I felt the call to come to Jesus.

> Just as I am
> Without one plea,
> But that Thy blood
> Was shed for me,
> O Lamb of God,
> I come, I come.

All around me boys and girls my age were feeling the call. They would rise from their seats and stumble to the altar and kneel in tears. They would whisper in the preacher's ear; he would give them a hug then go on to the next soul.

There was one girl in our church who got saved every time there was a revival. If there was a week-long revival she might get saved three or four times a week. How I envied those lucky souls who had been touched as they knelt there, their shoulders racked with sobs as the minister heard their confessions and gave them salvation.

And then I began to consider an alternative. What if I could buy salvation! What if when the Devil came to throw me into the Eternal Fire I was able to say that I had given my fortune to the church. The thought gave me momentary peace.

It may have been the newfound peace that caused me to revert to my willful and ignoble nature. Was it necessary, I asked myself, to donate the entire quarter to the collection box? What if I tithed? Would ten percent buy full salvation, or only a percentage? Looking for any excuse to hold on to as much of the money as I could, I did the arithmetic and calculated that ten percent of twenty-five is two and a half cents. How could I donate ten percent? Who by rights should get the half-cent, God or me?

I might have done the decent thing and given God

his full due had it not been for a chance visit to the city. Like many a country boy before me, the temptations of the big city were overpowering.

All these many years later I cannot visit Charlottesville, Virginia, without remembering what became of Myrle's quarter, and how I fell even further from grace.

❁   ❁   ❁

Sometimes on my way home to Nelson County from California, I fly to Dulles Airport, rent a car, and drive down Route 29. It is a lovely drive through old towns where the lights are just beginning to come on for the night. State historical markers point out where this or that Civil War battle took place.

At Manassas the old fought-on landscape is dotted with cannon and fencerows, and ghosts lurk in the shadows. As dusk begins to fall, the Blue Ridge Mountains come into view, and my heart lifts. At such an hour the mountains are fringed with rich crimson sunsets that fade gradually to purple and then to a dark blue.

I stop in Charlottesville, park my car, and walk along the Mall where once Main Street was busy with street cars, country people, horse drawn wagons, and buggies.

It is usually late at night by the time I arrive there, and I go looking for the boy I used to be. He is twelve years old, and he has a quarter burning a hole in his pocket.

He is tall for his age, a freckled boy wearing knickers, mended many times at the knees, ankle socks in a brown argyle pattern worn thin at the heels, and his "good" shoes which have been freshly polished in observance of this trip into the city. It is the third year of use for the "aviator" jacket he wears, and since he has grown alarmingly in the past year his wrists stick out inches below his sleeves. His short sandy colored hair is covered by an imitation leather "aviator" cap that fits snugly around his head.

He is a country boy in town, so he moves tentatively. This is Albemarle County, after all, and foreign country. By nature the boy is shy, but he is also unsure of himself because he doesn't know city ways.

People move more briskly here than they do out in the country. Everybody is nicely dressed. Many of them are students at the University, wearing saddle shoes and good tweed jackets.

The boy stands in front of the Woolworth Five-and-Dime, his nose pressed against the glass. He feels the quarter in his pocket. He tells himself that he must not spend it, but his will is weakening. It would buy several Big Five writing tablets, and he needs a new one for the journal he is keeping. Secretly he yearns to be a writer and has kept a journal almost from the time he first learned to write. The quarter would also buy a pair of socks. He needs them badly. He enters Woolworth intent on simply pricing the socks. On the way to the sock counter he passes Stationery. Almost in a trance he selects a tablet, hands over the quarter, and receives fifteen cents in change.

All caution, all conscience has been thrown aside. Back on Main Street, carrying his tablet in a sack, he wanders. In front of Timberlake Drug Store he stops. He has never ventured in, but he has always wanted to see what it is like inside. Recklessly he enters. A waiter indicates a round marble-topped table and indicates it is free. The boy sits uncomfortably in one of the wrought-iron chairs. A couple at the next table are sharing with straws something dark and interesting looking.

The waiter arrives and asks to take his order. The boy is confused by the menu, and finally he points to the couple at the next table and says, "What's that they're drinking over there?"

"Chocolate malt," answers the waiter.

"Can I have one of them, too?"

"Coming up."

The waiter disappears and the boy attempts to look as citified as the other customers, but he is ill at ease and his posture becomes withdrawn as if he is trying to become invisible. He fixes his eyes on the marble top of the table in front of him and waits.

But then his order arrives and a look of the purest

pleasure spreads across his thin, freckled face. In a single moment in those pinched and poverty-stricken days, this Young Prince of the Baptist church has given in to yet another temptation. The Devil has won! The boy has spent all but a nickel on drink.

It is his first chocolate malt. The rich, smooth, frosty, malty, chocolate creaminess of it is more delicious than anything he has ever imagined. He will remember it all the days of his life, and he will remember it in Hell where there is no doubt he is soon to become a citizen.

THE GIFT OF EDUCATION

Three Sisters: Nora Spencer Hamner—Aunt
Margaret Hamner Myers—Aunt
Lottie Hamner Dover—Aunt

Three of my father's sisters were generous to me beyond measure. I will always remain grateful to each of them, but the one aunt who made it all possible was the eldest of them, Nora Spencer Hamner.

There were eleven children in my father's family. My grandfather, Walter Clifton Hamner, suffered infantile paralysis in midlife and was wheelchair-bound for the rest of his days. My grandmother, Henry Spencer Hamner, who was said to have been named Henry because her father wanted a boy, was a resourceful wife. After my grandfather fell ill, she opened a boarding house for the workers at the soapstone-quarrying plant that supported our village.

Lilly, the oldest and reported to be the most beautiful of the women, died early. The next daughter was Nora. After a brief stint in nursing school she became

Nora Spencer Hamner

a "nurse on horseback." This was back in the 1920s when medical attention was rarely available in rural areas. When there was a serious illness, a scalded child, a breach birth, a slow death from tuberculosis, the patient suffered and died at home. Nora took her knowledge of medicine into the hills and hollows of the Blue Ridge and brought what medical knowledge she knew to those who otherwise might have died or suffered needlessly.

She was a handsome woman, and unconventional for her time. In a day when it was frowned on for women to wear slacks or to smoke cigarettes, she did both. Whenever I think of her I see her in the driver's seat of her old "woody" station wagon, her russet-colored hair blowing in the breeze as she whipped along the Skyline Drive, always on the lookout for wildflowers that stood in the way of a bulldozer widening the roads to form the Blue Ridge Parkway.

She was once known to have held up the progress of a truck hauling debris while she removed several trilliums from the path of a bulldozer.

There were two other sisters who lived with her at 29 Willway Avenue in the west end of Richmond.

Aunt Lottie was an office manager at the Matell Insurance Company. She oversaw a large staff of women usually referred to as "my gals." She had made an unwise marriage while still in her teens, divorced in her twenties, and left with a daughter, Charlotte Anne, to raise on her own. Lottie had been the "baby" of the family, always pretty, a little vulnerable, a tiny bit vain, and always expecting to find that second man who would love her and take away the hurt of the first marriage. As the years advanced and the man she yearned for did not arrive she succumbed to alcoholism, but then proved to everybody her inner strength, for by the time she died she had accomplished twenty-eight years of sobriety.

Lottie Hamner Dover

The third sister was Margaret. She was the elegant one, a patrician, and tall, a long-legged beauty.

Margaret had been educated at "The Kleinburg Academy" in Schuyler. How it came about that a retired schoolmaster named Wayles and his wife and two sisters came to set up an academy for young people in the backwoods of our village I will never know. The rumor persists to this day that the family was descended from relatives of Martha Wayles, the wife of Thomas Jefferson, and who will say that they were not? Today in Schuyler along a narrow dirt road a little bridge crosses a creek. Up in the woods back from the bridge, ensnared in wild berry bushes and mountain laurel, is a stone chimney that is all that remains of the Academy.

After our doctor's wife, Mrs. Laura Horsley,

Margaret Hamner Myers

Laura Boyd Horsley

arranged for me to receive a scholarship to the University of Richmond, the question was how to manage all the challenges. Not having money to live in the dorm, where would I live? Having no savings how would I feed myself?

The three aunts came to my rescue. They had already taken in my paternal grandmother. Grandma Hamner had her own room and I was given a cot at the end of her bed, a desk, a chair, and rights to whatever bathroom happened to be free.

The three aunts probably had no idea of the task they had set out for themselves. I was fresh from the hills, and except for our senior-class trip to New York in an old school bus, I had never been more than forty miles from home.

At first I felt closer to Sally Royal than I did to anyone else who lived in the house. Sally Royal lived in a room in the basement and was the current "colored" girl that Nora had gone "up in the country" to get, to train, and to employ.

Sally was as unaccustomed to city life as I was. She was quite tall and walked with a proud, graceful stride. She wore no makeup and had a natural African beauty that made her appear, at least in my eyes, aristocratic.

Sally had been instructed to address me as "Mr." Earl and I think I was as uncomfortable with the appellation as she was. Often in a tense moment at the table, if she happened to be serving, she and I would exchange glances that said, "What are we doing here!"

These three ladies were proud members of the Daughters of the American Revolution (DAR) and The United Daughters of the Confederacy (UDC) and under their guidance my rough back-country manners improved. I learned to stand when a lady entered the room, to always say ma'am, to help a lady to her seat at the table, and to shower each night whether I needed it or not. This was a novel experience to a boy from the hills accustomed to taking a bath every Saturday night.

I balked at only one of the aunts' instructions. I was told to shave under my arms. I would be damned, even if I lost my free room and board, if I was going to play Samson to three Delilahs!

There was one undercurrent of tenseness in our lives. Uncle Clay was the youngest brother of the clan. A tall man with a classical nose, crinkly dark wavy hair, warm brown eyes, and a handsome face, Clay was married to the head nurse at an important Richmond hospital. Clay had only one fault. He was violently anti-Semitic, so when he visited, everyone had mixed feelings of joy and misgiving.

What complicated the situation was that Aunt Margaret was in love with Julian Meyers, and Julian was a Jew. Eventually Margaret ignored Clay's objections and married Julian. They were one of the handsomest, happiest, and most loving couples I have ever known.

What a ménage we were! On a typical evening, Margaret and Julian held hands in the den while they sipped their old fashions. Nora read garden books in her own room while Sally Royal rested in the kitchen in between fetching Nora her "toddies." Over in her own room Lottie applied acres of cold cream and ointments to her face, while Charlotte did her lessons at her desk in the corner. And in Grandma Hamner's room

Grandma sat in her rocking chair and crocheted, while I tried to understand the mysteries of Freshman Math, which to this day are beyond my comprehension.

I was a poor student and I quickly learned that Schuyler High School had been an inadequate preparation for college. I was passing English 1 and History 1; I was getting by in Spanish but failing Freshman Math miserably.

World War II happened along just in time to keep me from becoming a serious failure.

I received my draft notice, but no one in the family believed I would be accepted. I was underweight and six feet tall, all long skinny wrists, awkward, shy, and clumsy: an Ichabod Crane.

On the night before I was to report to the induction center, the family announced they would not say goodbye because there was no way the army would accept such an apparition.

I took the streetcar down to the induction center and took the physical. Perhaps it was an indication of the desperation of the need for soldiers that I quickly found myself a private in the United States Army, at Fort Lee, Virginia.

It was the last time I would enjoy the "high life" I had grown accustomed to at 29 Willway Avenue, Richmond, Virginia.

When I returned from my service in the army the aunts were generous enough to take me in again. Aunt

Nora continued to be a determining influence in my life. My goal of becoming a writer was well known by her and so she kindly sent me to see Bill Robinson, an editor at the *Richmond News Leader*.

Mr. Robinson informed me that he tried to hire veterans returning to their old jobs and unfortunately had no opening at the moment, but he did say, "You have a nice speaking voice. Have you ever thought of radio work?"

He sent me over to radio station WMBG, where with the title Production Apprentice I opened the front door each morning, swept out the place at night and learned that this was the world I had been looking for, this is where I belonged.

Radio WMBG led me to Cincinnati, where I graduated from college into a writing job. That led to NBC in New York, where I wrote radio scripts in the daytime and worked on a novel at night.

My first novel was called *Fifty Roads to Town*. It was a well-written book about Pentecostals (Holy-Rollers) and a week in the life of a Southern village. It was submitted to Random House on a Friday and accepted the following Monday.

It was to get me in trouble back at 29 Willway Avenue.

The book was not autobiographical. However, in the copy on the inside jacket the copywriter had written "a novel about the strange folkways of Earl

Hamner's own people." I took this to mean a book about the people in the community I came from. I did not intend it in any way to be about my personal family.

The novel came out to good notices and Random House sent advance copies to reviewers as well as a list of family and friends, including the Richmond aunts. Random House also flew me down to Richmond for an autograph session at Miller and Rhoads.

Aunt Margaret picked me up at the airport. I asked about the family, and Margaret said, "Everybody's fine except your Aunt Nora."

"What's wrong with Nora?" I asked.

"After she read your book she took to her bed," replied Margaret.

I should mention here a couple of things about my novel. The first thing to note is that in their worship service Holy-Rollers sometimes become quite violent, seized by a kind of religious fervor which causes them to dance and fling themselves around the room, sometimes coming to rest on top of objects such as the piano.

I should also mention that one of the characters in the book, a mentally challenged man, would urinate out of doors whenever he needed to empty his bladder.

Margaret let me off at 29 Willway, and I went straight up to Nora's room. Sure enough, she was in her four-poster bed with the lace canopy. The room was in semidarkness and the shades were drawn.

"Aunt Nora," I called, trying to hide the nervousness I felt. "It's Earl."

"Come here, darling," she said, "and give me a kiss."

I approached her bed and kissed her cheek. She took my hand and held it while she said, "I want you to know that no matter what you have done, you are still family, and we love you anyway."

"I'm a little confused," I replied.

"I've read your book, and about half of Richmond has too. Earl, nobody in the family has ever worshipped Our Maker by dancing on the piano, and no one in the family, as far as I know, has ever voided on the ground."

Nora did not remain bound to her bed for long. It was autumn, time to go up to her cottage at Montebello, right off the Skyline Drive, where the autumn leaves can cure almost any illness—even mischief of an ungrateful nephew.

Nora, Margaret, and Lottie gave me a tremendous gift. They sustained and nurtured me through the difficult breaking-away from my mountain home and people. It was a period of transition for me as I turned from an innocent boy into a more aware and assured young man. Without their generosity, guidance, and love I might never have left Schuyler.

And I am sorry I caused Nora to take to her bed, but I don't think I caused irreparable damage to the family reputation, and it might have comforted her to know that many years later the DAR awarded me a citation for my work in television.

THE GIFT OF A LANDMARK

Jeanine—Friend

How I came to own one of the most elegant and price-less landmarks in the city of Paris is a long story. It began in August of 1944 when I entered the city shortly after it had been liberated.

For several months I had been assigned to the 19th Replacement Depot stationed near Nantwich, a tiny hamlet with picturesque thatched roofs not far from Chester, in England. I visited the area not long ago and the whole area has changed. Today the estate, Oulton Park, where we were camped out is one of England's best-known racetracks.

While we GIs waited there to be shipped to France, we were instructed in the fine art of defusing land mines. The life expectancy of those who had learned this skill was something like twenty minutes on the battlefield. I decided I probably had not long to live and woke each morning suspecting that I would die the minute I set foot in France.

Finally two months after D-Day, it was our turn to

"replace" the forward troops, and we left behind the green fields of Oulton Park.

Those of us who were lucky landed at Omaha Beach. The fighting there was long over, but the price in American lives to take the beach was unspeakable.

Even two months after the momentous events of June 6, 1944, the presence of death hovered over the sandy beach that was still littered with the corpses of landing-craft and other half-submerged ships and equipment. We had crossed the Channel in a Liberian ship, a vessel so filthy that we were glad when the time came to toss our duffel bags overboard to the troop landing craft waiting down below.

Unlike our less fortunate brothers who had climbed overboard and descended to the carrier on rope ladders to fight their way ashore, this time the beach was secure. I suffered severe acrophobia, but managed to go over the railing and down the rope ladder with my eyes shut.

I was in France at last and I was prepared to give all for my country. In fact, I was convinced that there was a land mine with my name on it waiting there for me.

We proceeded from the beach into Normandy, keeping about three or four miles behind the front lines. We slept under hedgerows or in the protection of a wall if part of a house or village remained. I remember one city called St. Lo that had been reduced to rubble. The sound of gunfire was constant as were the sounds of the B-24s overhead as they commuted around the clock to Berlin and Munich and Hanover. Miraculously, my unit moved forward without engaging the enemy, arriving finally in the small town of Etampes. There we were able to set up our pup tents on the grounds of a château, and mercifully we were able to take showers in the caretakers' cottage. We were thirty miles south of Paris.

You do things alphabetically in the army, so naturally, my tent mate was named Hammond. He was kind of a sweet, unimaginative, innocent guy from Indiana, a fastidious man who never let a morning go by without shaving with water in his steel helmet.

When Hammond learned that I was a writer he confessed that writing was a chore for him and asked me to I write a letter to his wife. I pulled out a tablet and asked what he wanted me to say. He thought for a while and said to write down that he loved her. Realizing that this was all the help I was going to get from Hammond, I improvised.

It was such a romantic declaration of love that if there ever had been a doubt in his wife's mind of his devotion it was gone forever. I wrote several letters for him, becoming more and more lyrical with each one. I lost track of Hammond after the war, but I am certain that those letters cemented his marriage for all time.

One night, ten of us were roused from our bedrolls and ordered to take our duffel bags and board a wait-

ing six-by-six GMC truck. It was the kind of truck you
see in military convoys, covered with a camouflage material, with an opening at the rear allowing unlimited
view of the landscape we were traveling through.

At some point the darkness gave way to sporadic
lights and I realized that we were passing through a
city, and to my delight I realized that the city was
Paris. At least, I thought, I would see a little corner of
Paris before I die.

The truck came to a stop. We were ordered to dis-
mount and were welcomed by Sergeant Albert Ott,
the forbidding master sergeant of the 542nd Quartermaster Corps. As it turned out my records claimed
that I was qualified to be an Administrative NCO 502,
which meant basically that I knew how to type. To my
great fortune the 542nd needed a typist more than a
land-mine defuser.

My barracks turned out to be an apartment building in Auberviellers, a suburb out toward Le Borget
Airport. Until recently it had housed a company of
German WACS. The only signs of their occupancy
were framed photographs of Adolf Hitler on the walls
and copies of *Mein Kampf* in dresser drawers, where
hotelkeepers in America usually store Gideon Bibles.
It would be my home for the next two years.

The 542nd Quartermaster Corps had already performed duty in the UK prior to moving to France, and
it was already functioning by the time I was assigned

to it. I came to admire and respect the commanding officer, Captain Paul Van Ripper, and even though he intimidated me at first I grew to respect Master Sergeant Ott, who was the ranking non-com in the company.

As soon as I was able to obtain a pass I set out to explore Paris. It was a strange time to be in The City of Light. What a far cry from the city tourists visit today! Food was scarce. Meat, chicken, and eggs were extremely expensive if they were available at all.

Legendary people came and went.

There were reported sightings of Ernest Hemmingway and Marlene Dietrich. Gertrude Stein and Alice B. Toklas had returned to Paris and opened their saloon. American GIs were welcome to the Stein salon as were Picasso and other artists. Utilizing material she gathered from visiting American soldiers, Miss Stein produced a novel called *Brewsie and Willie*. Raymond Duncan, brother of the legendary Isadora, could frequently be seen on the streets dressed in the long white robes said to have been hand woven.

Marion Hargrove, author of *See Here, Private Hargrove* and who was to become my friend and the writer of some of the most innovative *Walton* episodes, was working at the offices of Stars and Stripes on La Rue Scribe.

Occasionally an open-air French truck would pass. Packed on the back were hollow-eyed, emaciated, shabbily dressed, dazed-looking men. They were called the *"retournés,"* the French citizens who had been sent to Germany to do forced labor.

Our offices occupied a second-floor corner of an enormous warehouse filled with Army clothing and various and sundry supplies. In addition to the military personnel, several English-speaking civilians were working there. An embittered old Frenchman who had worked for the Bank of Canada before the war was one of the bookkeepers. One gentleman had worked in the French film industry, one of the ladies was a White Russian princess, and one of the younger French women had been a member of the underground and had been a courier for the FFI, the French Resistance. But best of all there was Jeanine.

I will not use her real name because she may, I hope, still be alive, married to some nice old Frenchman, possibly a grandmother, and I doubt that she has told her husband that she once had a romance with an American soldier. During the occupation she had lived in Africa, where her father had practiced medicine.

She was beautiful the way Olivia de Havilland was beautiful in *Gone with the Wind*. She wore Chanel perfume and even in postwar Paris she dressed for work in clothing that had taste and style. I was attracted to her at once, but she was cautious.

A few American soldiers, while welcomed by most of the population, had earned a bad name for all of us. Passing through the city, often assuming correctly that they would not be coming back, many GIs had given vent to their fears and frustrations and longing. Often they had picked up a catchphrase in French for "Would you like to sleep with me?" And they had called it out indiscriminately to any female from nineteen to ninety. Many of the French assumed all of us American soldiers were, as the English claimed, "overpaid, oversexed, and over here!"

Although we worked together every day it was some time before Jeanine would agree to a date. I persevered and finally she named the place and time and even provided the tickets. It was to a concert at the Palais de Chaillot where Pierre Monteaux was conducting a cycle of all of Beethoven's symphonies.

Another even more memorable event Jeanine and I attended was the first post-war appearance of Edith Piaf. Jeanine explained that Piaf was revered by the French, was called "The Little Sparrow," and she spoke and sang about the "little" people of Paris.

The concert took place at the Olympia Theater and Piaf's appearance was preceded by a then-unknown, nineteen-year-old Italian named Yves Montand.

He was an electrifying performer. One of his songs, described in the program as a "chanson realistic," was accompanied by eloquent descriptive movements of his huge expressive hands:

> *Comme ce drolle*
> *Le gens qui marche dans la rue*
> *Come ce drolle*
> *Deux ceur perdue en la cohue*
> *Le serenade d'la amour*
> *Le serenade de toujour*
> *Et moi je suis la*
> *Pour le vire.*

Another of his songs he introduced as being a "chanson de cowboy," and it went something like:

> *Dans les pleins du far ousts*
> *Quand viens la nuit,*
> *Les cowboys dan leur bivouac*
> *Son reunite*
> *En bas de la ciel*
> *De Mexico*
> *Ils chant "Ei ei ei ei O"*

Many years later, after the war, I learned that Montand was going to give a concert in Los Angeles. I wrote to him in care of his American agent, telling him that I had attended that concert at the Olympia Theater and requesting that he include "The Cowboy

Song" and "La Chanson Realistic" in his concert. I was disappointed at the concert when he did not include either song, but decided that my letter had probably never reached him.

Almost a year later I received a note from Montand. He thanked me for remembering the Olympia performance and apologized, explaining that he had received my request too late to include the songs I had requested.

When Edith Piaf took the stage her appearance was stunning in its drama. All lights had been dimmed until the entire theater was in total darkness. From the pit came almost imperceptibly the muted sounds of *"La Vie en Rose."* As the music increased in volume, a single spotlight appeared, a dot on the curtain. The dot enlarged and grew larger until it became her face. By the end of *"La Vie en Rose"* the audience had risen as a single body as we roared our appreciation.

Jeanine also saw to it that I was introduced to the more cultural aspects of the city. She discovered that the Sorbonne was offering French classes to American soldiers. I enrolled and managed to learn a better grade of French than I had picked up in bars and from workers in the warehouse.

She became my guide to some of her favorite places in the city. She had been away from France for five years so it was a combination homecoming for her and a guided tour for me. Together we explored the bookstores along the Seine and the twisted little streets around La Sacre Coeur where artists were once again setting up their easels.

One especially memorable tour included a stop at what she called "my bridge." It was Le Pont Alexandre III, an elegantly arched bridge spanning the Seine boasting magnificent candelabra decorated with cupids and sea monsters. At either end of the bridge are groups of equestrian figures in gilded bronze. The Eiffel Tower is visible in the distance and small boats sail underneath. From any point of view it is breathtaking.

Meanwhile, my daily responsibilities to the army continued, and all was not well. There was constant, small-scale pilfering taking place in the warehouse. Most of the laborers in the warehouse were Algerians. From time to time one of them would be caught smuggling some small item of clothing out of the warehouse and was fired.

There was also more subtle stealing that took place. One of the female office employees showed up one day in a fashionable suit. It had style and looked like it might have come out of one of Paris's top fashion houses. In truth, it had been made out of a purloined olive-drab Army blanket. And it didn't look too bad either.

There was an old Frenchman who wore several hats around our office. He was a kind of liaison between the office and the warehouse, guiding supply sergeants to where their requisitions could be filled, emptying wastebaskets, and cleaning the office at the

Le Pont Alexandre III

end of the day. He was always willing to do whatever was required. He was especially fond of Jeanine and he never failed to stop to say good morning to her when she arrived.

His name was Monsieur Jean Prieu, and he was from the Basque region and spoke French with a "southern accent." Actually it was a blend of French and Spanish but it was nearly incomprehensible to the unfamiliar ear.

One morning he stopped by Jeanine's desk and then came by mine to say goodbye. He said some other things that I did not understand, which Jeanine translated. It seemed he had stolen a pair of socks and had been fired.

I asked him to stay for a moment while I went down into the warehouse and found the sergeant in charge. He agreed that Monsieur Jean was a worthy person, but that his instructions were to automatically fire anyone caught stealing. Somehow I convinced the sergeant to give the old guy a second chance. Monsieur Prieu was extremely grateful.

Soon after that Jeanine and I were invited to dinner at the Prieu home. The following Sunday we arrived at their modest apartment in La Rue de Gros Perroquet (the Street of the Fat Parrot).

Madame Prieu was a stout, red-faced, hearty lady who was totally outgoing and likeable. Her husband was a gracious host. He provided a bottle of wine and for dinner there was coq au vin. A lengthy description was given about how they had come by the chicken which involved Madame going by train out into the country to visit relatives who had done her the favor of selling one of their chickens to her.

The food was delicious and under the influence of the warming wine monsieur and madame confessed to a secret. They had abhorred the Germans. They had hated the occupation and had sworn that they would have revenge. They plotted at length and eventually lured a German soldier into a dark alley, where they murdered him. There was no mistaking their honesty or their pride.

Somehow this event led to Jeanine's finally inviting

me to visit her home and to meet her family. My cousin Curtis Giannini was on leave in Paris, and I invited him to go along. When I introduced him in my faltering French as "*mon cuisine*" (my kitchen), her parents seemed to decide that, trustworthy or not, I at least was good for a laugh. I don't think they ever trusted me completely, but at least the ice was broken.

After that Jeanine became "my girl." The first time I kissed her was on the Pont Alexandre III.

Interesting relationships developed between American soldiers and the French women. Some soldiers simply sought out prostitutes that were legal and available. Others seemed to make more personal arrangements. In our office one of our sergeants became engaged to and married his French sweetheart.

There was another man in my unit who had promised his wife back in America that he would be faithful to her until he came home. Still he dated the beautiful young Simone, one of the assistants in our office. He confessed when he said goodbye to me that on his last night before returning to the States he had broken his word to his wife.

Another of my friends, Fred, from New Hampshire, had some kind of relationship with a somewhat older lady. I never met her but Fred referred to her fondly as "Old Trente Sept." Fred and I had another friend who shipped out suddenly. He entrusted a package and a letter to us and requested that we deliver it to his girlfriend. The address he gave was in Pigalle.

When we found the address the woman who answered the bell was wearing an American corporal's medal on the front of her blouse. She seemed not surprised to find two American GIs on her doorstep and invited us in.

When we explained the mission we were on, our hostess explained that this address was not our friend's girlfriend's home because "she worked at night," but if we were interested two of her ladies were available and she could arrange a show. Fred and I fled, left the package, and hoped for the best.

News of the war on the German front continued encouraging, and on May 8th, 1945, victory in Europe was declared. In Paris the event was celebrated with huge crowds cheering and milling about on Les Champs Élysées. Jeanine and I were there. She wore an especially fetching hat and crowds of children took hands and danced circles around her chanting *"Le Chapeau."* Here and there in the crowds some people wept.

Gradually I became convinced that Paris was my spiritual home. There was some talk that many of us soldiers would be sent to fight the Japanese, but I promised myself that even if I were shipped there, I would come back to Paris once the war in Japan was over. This was where I wanted to spend the rest of my life. I planned to take my discharge overseas, collect my mustering-out pay, and finish the novel I now had in mind.

As it turned out, I did not have to go to Japan for I was still in Europe when that war ended.

I might have been there today, were it not for a movie called *State Fair*. The story is about as corny as it can get, about a family preparing for and going to the Iowa state fair to exhibit their prize pig. But it was in Technicolor and the sun shone with a warmth I had not experienced since I left Virginia. There were Dick Haymes and Jeanne Craine singing Rogers and Hammerstein tunes like "It's a Grand Night for Singing" and "It Might as Well Be Spring!" Even such ridiculous elements as Fay Bainter winning the best pickle contest did not distract from a growing conviction that by planning to settle in France, I was about to make a major mistake in my life.

When I came out of the theater, rain was still falling and the gray skies over Paris were grayer still. The French people I had so loved seemed suddenly shabby, disconsolate, and petty.

The tables at the sidewalk in front of Fouquets were all empty. I took the Metro to La Porte de la Villette and then walked up the Avenue d'Aubervillers until I came to the bar on the corner near our billet.

I went in and took a seat at the bar. The place was called "Le Café de les Communistes" and it was frequented mostly by guys from my unit and working-class men from the area. The proprietor knew me and knew what I liked and brought me the brandy in a snifter. As I sipped it I could see myself in the mirror. Looking at my image I had to look myself in the eye and the thing that kept going through my mind was, "Who are you fooling?"

Suddenly I didn't feel so grown up. I felt like a kid. I wanted sunshine. I wanted the sounds of American voices. I wanted to see my family. I wanted to see my mother's forsythia blossoming in her front yard. I wanted salty home-cured ham on a fresh-baked baking-powder biscuit dripping with yellow butter. I was the most homesick person in the Western world.

On the last night before I was to ship out, Jeanine suggested that we go to the bridge where I had first kissed her. I tried to explain that I was homesick, promised that I would be back, but I think she knew that we might never see each other again.

"I have a going away present for you," she said. "I am giving you my bridge."

And I kissed her for the last time on Le Pont Alexandre III. It is still the most beautiful bridge in the world.

And it is mine.

THE GIFT OF ENCOURAGEMENT

Mina Barton—Editor

I was expecting an impatient housewife to open the door. Instead, I was surprised and delighted when the woman who greeted me was not the least impatient, and was to have a far-reaching effect on my life.

It was soon after World War II, and I had enrolled in a writing class at the College of Music of Cincinnati. This fine school was in time to become known as the Media Division of the College of Music of the University of Cincinnati.

Even with the GI Bill paying part of my way it was necessary to take some kind of additional work. The job I found was called Newspaper Readership Testing. It required me to go through an assigned area in the suburbs, to knock on doors, and to ask the householder for permission to show them the morning paper, then turn each page and have them point out articles or advertisements they had noticed. For each interview I was paid fifty cents.

It took a certain amount of patience and kindness on the part of the person being interviewed. Many people did not take kindly to an odd-looking young man asking them to lay aside their housework or a crying baby just to point out some newspaper article they scarcely remembered. Sometimes a harassed housewife would simply slam the door in my face. Others would murmur "Busy" or "Sorry" and be gone.

It was discouraging work until one morning there came an event that was to have a profound effect. In answer to my knock a pleasant-faced middle-aged woman agreed to be interviewed. She came out of the house and we sat on the top step of her front porch. Prior to the interview I was required to write down the name and address of the respondent along with his or her occupation.

"I'm a magazine editor," the woman replied in answer to my query.

I was stunned. Editors to me were inaccessible people who lived in New York skyscrapers and spent their days signing rejection notes which they returned to writers like me, reading: "Thank you for submitting this manuscript. We are sorry but it does not meet our present needs."

"I'm a writer," I announced, overlooking the fact that at the moment I was canvassing a Cincinnati suburb at fifty cents a throw. She asked about my writing and I eagerly confessed to a lifelong desire.

I told her that I was in school at the moment, but that I dreamed of writing novels eventually.

For more than an hour Mina Barton sat and talked about writers and writing. She advised me to set aside a specific time for my writing so I would form the habit of writing. She suggested I find a "place" to write, somewhere I could be comfortable and with a minimum of interruption. She warned me to let nothing short of death come between me and my writing time.

She talked about keeping a journal, and I proudly revealed that I had kept such a record almost from the time I was in the third grade. And she talked about writing from the heart, about passion, and how if we write about something we feel passionate about that passion will convey itself to the reader. And finally she repeated what I had heard from every writing instructor and read in every how-to book: "Write about what you know!"

She asked if I had a book in mind. I told her about the book that I had been working on in one form or another. I had always been haunted by a poem written by Muriel Rukeyser. It is called "Effort at Speech Between Two People," and it dramatizes the yearning of a young girl to communicate, to reach out, to be heard, and to be understood. And I had found a perfect symbol for the idea.

At the Holy-Roller church back home, the worshippers at the height of religious ecstasy would burst into "the unknown tongue." It sounded like babble, but I have learned in later years that it is said to resemble certain ancient Arabic tongues.

I was fascinated by the "rollers" and the concept led me to conceive of my heroine as a young girl who yearned to communicate and who dreamed that if she could speak "the unknown tongue" it would give her the power to make herself known, to share her secrets, to end her loneliness, to give and receive love, to communicate with everybody in the world.

Mrs. Barton excused herself and went inside the house. When she returned she handed me a copy of *Writer's Digest*. (The magazine is still published in Cincinnati.) She opened the magazine to a page and showed me an article titled "Paradise on Five Dollars a Day."

I did not retire to "Paradise" immediately, but some years later I picked up a copy of the magazine that would one day change my life.

THE GIFT OF PARADISE

B. B. Caverly—Landlady

Every writer yearns for an inexpensive place where he can enjoy privacy and write without interruption. In other words, "Paradise."

I doubt that Mina Barton expected that I would actually go there when she showed me an article called "Paradise on Five Dollars a Day" in *Writer's Digest*, but the notion stayed in the back of my mind. Following my graduation from the University of Cincinnati I was given a job as a radio writer at WLW, the major radio station in the state.

It was a wonderful time in my life, a transition from student to professional writer. It was a time of growth, of learning, of falling in love and forming friendships that would last a lifetime. Cincinnati in those days had some of the most beautiful girls in the country, and I wanted all of them for my very own.

WLW paid handsomely, and I led a frugal life that allowed me to save a sizeable nest egg.

I once had the good fortune to interview Katherine

Anne Porter, and when I asked her to describe her writing process she said: "Somewhere out of travel, life, experience, the past, or just from imagination, an idea seizes me and won't let go. I don't act on it immediately, but put it away to cook. After a while faces, language, customs, traits, colors, events, all come together around that idea like iron filings around a magnet. Even then I don't begin writing, until one day the book tells me it is ready to be written, and that is when I begin."

I had reached that point. The novel I had dreamed of for years was clamoring somewhere in my brain demanding to be written.

I quit my job at WLW and rented a small cottage I found advertised in the *Writer's Digest* column: "Paradise on Five Dollars a Day."

I rented "Paradise" sight unseen through the mail from the owner, a lady named B. B. Caverly. The ad described a small stone cottage at the foot of Rich Mountain in the heart of the Ouachita Mountains of Arkansas. The ad went on to mention that the cottage had neither electricity nor indoor plumbing. To compensate for the lack of such amenities, Miss Caverly informed me that food has a special flavor when cooked over an open fire and there were fish in the stream nearby for the price of a worm.

One bit of information omitted from the ad was any mention of the fact that passage to the cottage meant one had to walk across the trunk of a tree that had fallen across the stream and the stream below was alive with cottonmouth moccasins.

I traveled by bus to the small town of Mena, Arkansas, and spent the first night in a charming little hotel called The Antlers. In the lobby were pictures of Chet Lauck and Norris Goff, who played "Lum and Abner" on one of radio's best-loved, longest-running shows. I had grown up listening to the show on NBC and was thrilled to actually be close to the country and the people they had so lovingly portrayed.

The two men not only created the show but also were writers, producers, and actors voicing all the characters. Chet Lauck played Lum, Grandpappy Spears, and Cedric. Goff portrayed Abner, Squire Skimp, and Dick Huddleston. Today their comedy might appear quaint and dated, but it was firmly rooted in the folk and folklore of their region and was said to receive more fan mail than any other radio show of its time.

On the morning following my night at the Antlers Hotel, my new landlady, Miss B. B. Caverly called for me. There was a Texas twang in her speech and her dark hair and chinquapin eyes made me think she might be partly American Indian. Many people in that part of the country do have Indian ancestry and will quickly and proudly upon meeting you tell what percentage Osage or Cherokee or Comanche blood runs in their veins.

Over breakfast Miss Caverly explained that the little town of Mena was named for Queen Wilhelmina of the Netherlands. Before the turn of the century a railroad company had built a magnificent hotel and resort at the top of a nearby mountain. Because many of the investors were Dutch, the resort was named the Wilhelmina Inn.

At the time of our breakfast, that resort hotel had been deserted and had fallen in ruins. In its place today the state has built another resort, the Queen Wilhelmina Lodge, which is a major tourist attraction in the region.

I checked out of the Antlers Hotel feeling just a little nervous about what I had committed myself to. We stopped at a small grocery where Miss Caverly waited while I purchased some supplies.

Miss Caverly then drove me a distance out of town. She parked her pickup truck on the roadside and led the way down a narrow path through the underbrush. I carried my duffel bag and some groceries. She carried my portable typewriter. We crossed an abandoned railroad track, presumably all that remained of the one the Dutch investors had built. Weeds grew up to our knees between the rusted rails and the rotting wooden ties.

Past the old railroad she led me to a fallen tree, which was the only access to the other side of a small creek. I scrambled after her and made it successfully to the other side where a six-foot-long black snake reared up in the path ahead.

I recoiled, ready to abandon "Paradise" and retreat to Mena and civilization, but the lady said, "Don't be scared. It's a good snake. They eat the bad ones."

Comforted slightly I followed her up the mountain to the cottage. It really was as charming as promised. I was told it had been built by a Belgian artist named Menti or Benti, I was never sure. It had been constructed, with an artist's sensibility, of native stone. There was a wide veranda across the front that afforded a fine view facing Rich Mountain. There was a kitchen, a living room, and a bedroom. A suitable distance out in the woods was an outhouse and in the side yard was the cooking facility, a barbeque grill made out of the same native stone as the house.

Before she left, Miss Caverly suggested that I not go out after dark, or if I did to carry a strong flashlight. She had neglected to tell me that the cottage was in the middle of something called "a snake run." She explained that the snake population at the summit of the mountain had no water supply, and they came down to the creek whenever they got thirsty, and that the cottage happened to be right smack in the middle of their path.

At that point it crossed my mind that I might be sacrificing my life in order to write this book, but I bravely decided to risk at least one night in "Paradise" before returning to civilization.

Miss Caverly was an ideal landlady. She would come by from time to time to check on me or to drop off food, but she knew I wanted privacy and she granted it to me.

I grew used to being a hermit. I received my mail by walking over to a box on the highway, and I hiked into town once in a while when supplies ran low. I made the trip only when I had to because of the long walk into town. But even more daunting, it required me to walk across that fallen tree and risk falling into the moccasin-infested water.

As primitive as my cottage was, it provided a perfect atmosphere in which to write. It was so isolated that except for Miss Caverly I had no human visitors. Occasionally a deer would wander across the property or a cottontail would hop by going about its business. There was no telephone, and the only sounds were songs from a variety of birds that came and went.

By the end of that summer I had finished almost half of the manuscript that was to become *Fifty Roads to Town*. It was to become my first published book and to this day I have Mina Barton to thank for guiding me to Miss Caverly and "Paradise on Five Dollars a Day."

Postscript: A few summers ago I attended a writer's conference in Tulsa, Oklahoma. After the conference was over I rented a car and drove down to Arkansas to visit my old haunt. Fifty years had passed since I had lived there. The small town of Mena had grown into a thriving tourist Mecca, but the people were the same kind and considerate folks I had first met at the Antler's Hotel. When I finally found my old cottage I hardly recognized it. Someone had bought it and "improved" it by adding electricity and a second story, but the view of the mountains was still the same, and the memories of my time there came back rich and sweet.

My only regret was that Miss Caverly was nowhere to be found, and I could not thank her for my sojourn in "Paradise."

THE GIFT OF THE BIG TIME

Dorothy McCann—Producer

This is a story—actually it's a confession—about a man who betrayed a friend, brought distress and disappointment to a woman who had been extremely generous to him and deserved nothing but gratitude. The friend was Mrs. Dorothy McCann, wife of Harrison McCann of the McCann Erickson Advertising Agency. The despicable person who betrayed her trust and brought her grief was I!

I had spent the summer working on a novel, and while I had a good portion of the manuscript down on paper I had not held a paying job in a while and was becoming more and more penniless every day.

My sister Marion's wedding to Glenn Hawks called me back to Virginia. I was happy to be home and to be with my family, but I wanted desperately to get back to work on the book. That would be impossible. I was broke and had to find a job.

When I had a chance for a free ride to New York with a friend, Joyce Payne Pierson and her husband,

I accepted the offer gladly.

Joyce and her husband were kind enough to offer me their guest room until I could find permanent accommodations. Even though I had known Joyce all her life and their hospitality was most sincere, I felt I had already imposed on the Piersons enough so I began looking around for other accommodations. An apartment of my own was out of the question, but I did find a single room for rent on West 96th Street in a flat leased to a Viennese psychologist and his wife. They were decent people and did not press for the rent even when I went days and weeks beyond the date the rent was due.

One of the first people I called on during my job search was Van Woodward, head of the writing staff at NBC. Getting through on the phone to Van was quite easy. He, too, was an alumnus of WLW. A mutual friend, Dave Brown from Cincinnati, had already paved the way, and Van greeted me cordially in his Rockefeller Center office.

Van and I became good friends right away. He respected good writers, and I came recommended as having some talent. Van took me in his confidence and told me a dilemma he was facing. He had a writer on staff that was drinking heavily and could not carry his share of the load. Van did not have the heart to fire the man, but he was doing everything he could to find him another job. Once he located a job for the writer, Van said, he would like to hire me as his replacement. Would I wait?

I was delighted at the prospect of becoming a member of the NBC writing staff eventually, but in the meantime I needed immediate income.

Christmas was not far off and I was able to find a part-time job as a clerk in the toy department at Macy's.

I had met Dorothy McCann a year or two earlier. She was the producer of a radio show called *Dr. Christian*. When I called she cordially invited me to drop by. Mrs. McCann was an attractive woman. Her soft, pink complexion was set off by beautiful snow-white hair and deep-blue eyes. Her corner office at 29 Rockefeller Plaza was elegantly but tastefully furnished, and she made me most comfortable.

Dr. Christian was a popular show which advertised itself as "the only show on radio where the audience writes the scripts."

It was not a misstatement. Each year thousands of speculative scripts arrived in Mrs. McCann's office. As might be expected, many of them were amateurish, but many of us who were fledgling writers submitted scripts also.

The scripts were judged by professional writers and editors, and many of them were chosen for broadcast. Several of the best scripts were given prizes, and a year earlier I had received one of the top monetary

awards. Being one of the winners meant being invited
to New York and participating in a special radio program honoring the lucky writers. Other winners included Rod Serling and John McGreevey. Both men
were to become friends in later years.

Dr. Christian was played by Jean Hersholt, a distinguished Hollywood actor. The stories were all set in
the small town of River's End, USA, and Dr. Christian was assisted by his nurse, Judy Price, played by
actress Rosemary DeCamp. The show's sponsor was
Vaseline Petroleum Jelly.

Mrs. McCann held my prize-winning script in high
regard. It was called "Who Would Not Sing for
David?" and it told the story of a veteran of World
War II who had given his life for his country and was
given the opportunity to visit his hometown for one
last look before entering heaven. In the script I tried
to convey how I might have felt if I had to spend one
final visit to my own hometown. It was an emotional,
heart-warming show, and Mrs. McCann told me that
the show had brought in more audience mail than any
other show she had ever produced. Especially gratifying was that many of the letters were from mothers,
wives, and sweethearts of veterans who had died in
combat.

When she learned that I was selling toys at Macy's
she said, "We can do better than that." She went on to
say that she knew I did not intend to become an ad-

vertising writer but that she was willing to hire me as an apprentice until I could find a more suitable writing position. Besides, she added, a little knowledge of advertising never hurt anybody.

It was more than generous of her. I was given an office, a small one but a long way from where I had been a month before. I had been suffering abject poverty but now I had moved into "the big time!"

Mrs. McCann's secretary, a nice woman named Rita Franklin, took me around and introduced me as "the new apprentice." I felt a little like "the teacher's pet!" But I didn't care. I was eating better and I quickly found and moved into an apartment on West 87th Street.

Knowing that I was Mrs. McCann's protégé, the others on the staff took some pains to actually teach me the ropes, and I learned a great deal.

When the scripts began to arrive for that year's *Dr. Christian* contest, Mrs. McCann assigned me to the judging panel. The panel consisted of an interesting group of writers. One of the ladies, a mystery writer, entertained us with original songs. I remember one, which she sang with a great deal of feeling:

> From my lover's lips
> Drips
> Blood!
> In my lover's eyes

Dries
Blood!
No more poems to me'll be wrote,
For I have cut
My lover's throat!

Another of the male judges came back from lunch every day under the influence of several martinis, and a lady novelist whose career had faded years before would issue an invitation to us male writers to "come by my place after work," making it fetchingly clear what might happen.

Some of the scripts were really bad and after reading so many of the unintentionally amusing ones, someone came up with the idea that each of the judges write a parody.

In my parody, I changed Dr. Christian's name to Dr. Pious. His nurse, Judy Price, became Nudie Rice, and I changed the location of River's End to River Bottom, USA.

The script opened with Dr. Pious and his nurse "hassling" on the gurney. They were interrupted by people with different ailments, which Dr. Pious would identify as "Canker of the Withers" or "Pyromania" or "Incest Burn." And for each ailment Dr. Pious would prescribe generous doses of Vaseline Petroleum Jelly.

Somehow copies of the parodies the judges wrote got loose in the building. I noticed that Mrs. Mc-

Cann's greeting had become curt and distant when I ran into her on the elevator.

I suspected what might have happened and Rita Franklin confirmed that her boss had indeed read the parody and was not amused.

Fortunately, soon after that Van Woodward found another job for his alcoholic writer and asked me to join the NBC writing staff.

I went to say goodbye to Mrs. McCann. She was cool at first, but thawed a bit and wished me good luck.

I thought we had seen the last of each other, and there was always an uneasy feeling whenever I looked back on the entire episode.

And then one day a year or so later she called me over to her office. Not a word was said of my unfortunate parody. She greeted me warmly and enthusiastically telling me of her intention to turn *Dr. Christian* into a television series and that she wanted me to write the pilot.

In preparation I spent an afternoon with her and her husband exploring a location on Long Island. We were scheduled to meet again to discuss the project when I learned that she and her husband had tragically been killed in an automobile accident on the Long Island Freeway.

THE GIFT OF LOVE

Jane Martin Hamner—Wife

"I want to make it clear that I am never going to get married!"

I would make that idiotic, sappy, sophomoric announcement to any unfortunate young lady I was dating who seemed to be taking a more than passing interest in our relationship.

In my lofty, self-important stupidity I would boast that I was a successful young novelist who had an "obligation" to supply to "my public" those novels, short stories, essays and memoirs for which those millions of readers hungered and thirsted! It is a wonder any intelligent young woman would go out with me for a second time, and I suspect I actually did miss getting to know a good many nice young ladies because of my conceit.

I would announce that as soon as the royalties from my first book started pouring in I would move to Paris. I confess to my shame that I made this announcement even before my first book had been published. Perhaps I could be forgiven for my youth and ignorance, and also because I had lived in Paris during and after World War II and had fallen in love with the city as so many other writers and artists before me had done. In my fantasy I knew precisely that little Left Bank attic studio I would rent. I would write my bestsellers at night. I would take early morning strolls along the quay beside the Seine. I already knew some French, but I would study the language and become proficient. I would cultivate knowledge of French wines. I would wear a beret.

It was in 1954 and I was working at the time as a radio writer at the National Broadcasting Company in Rockefeller Center. One evening, as is the custom in New York City, I made a date for drinks after work and went to join my friends Ed and Sherry Keen. I had known the Keens in Cincinnati, where Ed was an actor and Sherry had been working at *Writer's Digest*. On my way to the table where the Keens waited I stopped to say hello to an acquaintance, Sue Salter, a publicist at NBC. Sue was an up-and-coming young career woman. She knew all the important people in the entertainment business and was already representing several celebrities.

Sue was beautiful. She looked a lot like the French actress Simone Signoret and she had an appealing way of finding everything in the world "divine!" Often an incident, an event, a party, a song, or a person was so "divine" that word came out: "deviiiii-innne!" And it usually was.

"I'd like you to meet my roommate, Jane Martin," said Sue. She introduced me to the most beautiful woman I had ever seen. Her blue-green eyes lit up with a smile that warmed the room. She was gorgeous. She was blonde. My heart stopped.

"I've just finished reading your book," said Jane.

I have no idea what I said in reply. She tells me that I stammered something. What I do remember is that when I reached Ed and Sherry's table, I said, "I've just met the girl I'm going to marry."

That was in February. I never again made my foolish announcement about remaining single. I began worrying about my future and whether I could support a wife. The little garret apartment on the Left Bank was quickly forgotten.

Jane and I started dating and a real relationship developed. As we became better acquainted we found more and more areas of mutual interest. We both loved The Village and movies and jazz and autumn leaves and Mabel Mercer and we both loved New York with the passion that comes from having been born somewhere else. She loved dogs and we both mourned the tragic death of Stormy, a cocker spaniel who was devoted to Jane and to Jane alone. She liked my friends and I liked hers.

I learned that Jane and Sue had come to New York

Jane Martin

from Davenport, Iowa. Jane had attended school in Davenport and graduated from Ward-Belmont, the school in Nashville that is known today as Harpeth Hall. She then went on to graduate from the University of Iowa. Together Jane and Sue had become the nucleus of a group of aspiring writers, artists, actors, and lawyers, most of them from the Midwest, and each of them firm in the knowledge that fame and fortune were just up ahead. They gave crazy, crowded

BYOB parties filled with young people bedazzled by New York and youth and talent and promise.

Jane had started her New York career doing office work for the Yellow Cab Company where drivers would come to blows over which one would get to drive her home after work.

When I met Jane she was working as an editor at *Harper's Bazaar*. I had an old Ford convertible in those days, a foolish luxury, but it did afford us transportation every weekend to a cottage I rented at a place called Lost Lake. It was in upper Westchester County not far from Danbury, Connecticut. Mutual friends would join us there and life was one grand party until Monday morning when we would have to return to work and reality.

An essential part of the courting process in those days was "meeting the parents." We drove to Davenport, where Jane's family had lived for generations in a beautiful Victorian mansion overlooking the Mississippi. As a matter of fact, when the house went out of Jane's family it became a bed and breakfast and can be seen on the Internet at www.fultonslanding.com.

Jane's maternal family were Scots. They had emigrated from a small coal-mining village called Wanlockhead in the southern highlands. Industrious and enterprising people, they became coal miners in a small Illinois village and within a few years not only owned the town but also had changed its name to their own.

Jane's father was Irish, a doctor, and a veteran of World War I. When I arrived on my quest for Jane's hand in marriage, the clan was pretty much ruled by the patriarch of the family, Uncle Hugh.

A dinner was arranged, and most of the clan showed up. Jane's brother, a doctor in Albany, New York, had come home for the big event. Chuck and I had already met in New York and he would give me a sympathetic and supportive look once in a while as I was being looked over by one or another of the uncles.

Finally it was Uncle Hugh's turn to cross-examine me. All the ladies had gathered after dinner in the green room. All the men congregated on the side porch and cigars and cigarettes were lit. Uncle Hugh looked at me and said, "I understand you are from an old Virginia family."

Whenever I become nervous or when there is a tense moment I tend to become ridiculously Southern. Therefore, my reply to Uncle Hugh sounded something like: "Yess sah, we been thar 'bout as long as anybody else has."

Even so, Uncle Hugh kindly gave his blessing, and we heaved a sigh and turned to face our next ordeal: meeting my family.

I too come from a clan, but it is larger than Jane's. We drove down to Virginia, and from night to morning we made the rounds of aunts, uncles, and cousins, first, second, and third.

We were married on October 16, 1954 in St. Bartholomew's Cathedral in New York. The reception was wonderful with all those sweet old reserved, conservative people from Iowa and Baptist, hill-country Virginians drinking champagne and getting acquainted. Jane and I had such a good time someone had to remind us when it was time to leave.

Of all the generous women I have known Jane has been the most generous and has given me the most precious gifts: a son, Scott, and a daughter, Caroline. And she has given me and continues to give me love that evidences itself in companionship, friendship, support, and intimacy. She is the best cook I know. Throughout our married lives she fed the children and me gourmet meals three times a day. Recently though, she announced that after fifty years she no longer plans to cook every meal and we must learn to "order in."

Jane has a reverence for life that is matched only by that of Dr. Albert Schweitzer, and she is still the most beautiful woman I have ever seen. For all of her becoming qualities, she has one major character flaw. She is unable to turn away any person who is hungry, and she cannot bring herself to ignore any animal in pain or without a home. Such is her reverence for life that she cannot even bring herself to throw away a houseplant that died months ago but still seems to have some vestige of life in it, and might recover, if fed, watered, and nurtured.

Jane Martin Hamner

I have to confess that this failure in her character gives me a certain amount of security. I am old now, a bit wilted and lumpy and rarely blossom anymore. So like her needy houseplant, I feel secure in the conviction that she won't throw me away either.

The one thing that Jane refuses to do is to read an unpublished manuscript because she does not want to be like Mrs. Samuel L. Clemens and "censor" my work. Therefore, she will be reading these words for the first time after the book is published, and it is quite possible that she will divorce me for revealing so much about a very, very private person.

As our fiftieth wedding anniversary approached all our friends kept asking, "How are you going to celebrate it?"

The questions seemed to demand that we celebrate in some grand manner. So we reacted by considering a cruise around Scandinavia, a theater orgy in London, or a visit to the Galapagos.

Finally we had to face the fact that none of these things seemed right. What we really wanted to do was to spend a week in New York with our children.

Caroline joined us from Laguna Beach. Scott came down from Bennington and we spent a week at the Algonquin.

It was just the right thing to do.

THE GIFT OF THE BIG EASY

Frances Parkinson Keyes—Novelist

The show was scheduled to be a two-hour live remote pickup from New Orleans. There were forty-five minutes left before we were to go on the air. Suddenly a twenty-minute segment was in trouble and we had nothing to fill it with. Twenty minutes to fill on a live show! It was disaster time!

The show was called *Wide Wide World*, one of NBC's most innovative quality shows. Dave Garroway, the first of the distinguished hosts of *The Today Show*, hosted it. Garroway was a genial man, an excellent talk show host. In person he was extremely intelligent, always well informed and considerate of his colleagues. His dark-rimmed glasses gave him a slightly owlish air and his unique sign-on or sign-off was to raise his hand and sing the single word *peace*.

Wide Wide World was broadcast two hours every Sunday afternoon during which the viewer could see events, interviews with newsworthy people, or visits to fascinating locations around the world. One week we would feature a concert in Boston, a sightseeing tour of the Grand Canyon, a tour of the White House, and/or a fishing trip off the Florida Keys.

Once in a while a single city or event would be featured. And when an in-depth visit to the city of New Orleans was scheduled I was assigned to write the script. The entire two hours was to be devoted to that single city. Research could not have been more pleasant, for it demanded that I spend nearly five weeks in The Big Easy visiting historical sites, exploring the port of New Orleans, spending time at Preservation Hall and eating my way from breakfast at Brennan's to dinner at Antoine's.

Eventually we settled on several different elements: a visit to a plantation with the haunting name of "Shadows on the Teche" and its owner, a courtly old gentleman named Weeks Hall; a visit to a farm where neutra, an animal raised for its fur, were raised; a stopover at a sulfur-mining ship; and a ride in a paddlewheel steamer featuring an interview with a harbor guide.

One of the most interesting segments to me was an interview with the legendary author, Frances Parkinson Keyes. Mrs. Keyes was the immensely prolific author of fifty-one novels. Her most famous novel was a mystery called *Dinner at Antoine's*, built around a murder that takes place in New Orleans just before Mardi Gras. Mrs. Keyes had traveled widely and had been married most of her life to a senator. When he died she established a writing center at historic Beauregard House in New Orleans and moved there to live.

John Goetz, the location producer, and I "called on" Mrs. Keyes at 1113 Chartres Street. Beauregard House had been built in 1826, but it had fallen in disrepair until 1940 when Mrs. Keyes formed a foundation for its restoration. General Pierre Gustav Toutant Beauregard and his wife had rented quarters in the house for an eight-month period after the Civil War. It was General Beauregard who ordered the shelling of Fort Sumter in Charleston, South Carolina, which is recognized as the signal for the beginning of the Civil War.

I was in awe of Mrs. Keyes. That she had written fifty-one bestsellers was impressive enough! She was also quite regal in her posture and especially considerate of me when she recognized my Virginia accent and learned that I had been born only twenty-four miles from her own birthplace of Charlottesville, Virginia. When I confessed that I was working on a novel, it led to an additional bond between us.

Some prose writers are often dismissive or even contemptuous of television. Mrs. Keyes simply stated that she did not have time to watch it. However, she did occasionally tune in to *The Today Show* for the news and was especially fond of "Mr. Galloway," as she called Dave Garroway. She was especially interested to learn that "Mr. Galloway" would be conducting the interview with her, and I think it was that promise more than anything else that persuaded her to agree to our barging into her drawing room with our camera crews.

On the day of the broadcast those of us on staff gathered in a control room at the NBC studios at Rockefeller Center. We would serve as the nerve center for the many different crews and cameras moved through their locations in New Orleans.

Barry Wood, executive producer of the series, was in place. A brisk, authoritative man, Barry had been a singer on the vintage radio music show called *Your Hit Parade* before going into production. He was known for his repertory of foul language. The in-studio staff went through a preliminary check to see if we were all in our places and knew what we were doing.

Actually, my work was all finished, but I wanted to be on hand for the outcome of weeks of research, writing, and preparation. Suddenly there came a frantic call from the Location Producer, John Goetz, in New Orleans.

"We've got a problem," John's voice came over the speakerphone. He sounded as if he was trying to remain calm, but a tremor in his voice betrayed his frustration.

"Mrs. Keyes has decided not to go along," he said.

"What the hell do you mean Mrs. Keyes has decided not to go along?" screamed Barry.

"She claims we deceived her. She thought Dave Garroway was coming to see her at Beauregard House. She was under the impression he was going to come by for tea and then she was going to show him around the place. She didn't know he was going to be in New York."

Barry got on the phone and I cringed as I recognized his use of the threat of lawsuit and other unpleasant events as he attempted to cajole the lady into doing his bidding. His voice level and the use of expletives grew in volume, and I could tell that Mrs. Keyes was not giving an inch. He went from phony-polite to obscene rage within minutes. Finally Barry screamed: "You got along with this old bitch when you were down there. Talk to her!"

I realized he was addressing me.

"I don't expect there's much I can do," I said.

"You want to keep your job?" he hollered.

"Sure do," I said.

"Then talk sense to the damned old broad."

I went into an adjoining office and picked up the phone extension. I was unaware that in the control room my voice was now on the speakerphone, and everything I said was being heard by my colleagues.

"Mrs. Keyes," I began. "This is Earl Hamner and I am sorry for this misunderstanding."

"Mr. Hamner," she said, "I have been in tears. This is the first time I have wept in many, many years."

"I am so very sorry to hear that," I said. "I apologize for the pain we have put you through."

"Mr. Hamner," she said. "In all my life I have never been addressed as Mr. Wood addressed me."

"He's not a gentleman, Mrs. Keyes," I said. "He just doesn't know how to talk to a lady."

"He threatened me, you know. I may have to take legal action."

"Oh, I wouldn't let him bother you that much," I said. "And please don't let one bad apple spoil this experience for you. He doesn't represent our industry. He is not a gentleman."

"He is vulgar," she said.

"Mrs. Keyes, I was wondering if you would reconsider doing the interview. It would be a personal favor to me."

"How so?" she asked.

"I could lose my job over this," I lied. "They will claim I misled you."

"Why would you want to continue working with such a contemptible man?" she asked.

"It's only to make enough money so I can write full time," I lied.

There was a long silence, long enough for my Baptist conscience to cause my whole face to redden with shame.

"Then if it's that important to you, I'll do it," she answered.

I hung up the phone and returned to the control room, where the opening credits were just beginning to roll. Sympathetic eyes rested on me. Except the eyes of Barry Wood.

"You freaking bastard," he shouted. "I ought to fire your ass!"

"Maybe," I said. "But I saved your show!"

And it went off without a hitch. When it came to her segment Mrs. Keyes was a trooper, poised and regal, as warm a hostess as I have ever seen, responding graciously to questions and comments from "Mr. Galloway" as warmly as if he were right there in the same room.

THE GIFT OF LITERATURE

Mabel Wheaton—Thomas Wolfe's Sister

While this book is primarily about generous women, I want to talk first for a moment about a generous man.

I met him in 1943 on a troop train when I was being transferred from one army post to another. At Fort Knox, Kentucky, I had been struggling to master the control of a six-by-six GMC truck in the mud of the Kentucky back country. It was too much for me. The truck won. I still hold the record for having gotten a vehicle the most deeply mired in the mud of any GI who ever managed to live though training in that God-forsaken place.

Having failed my contest with the truck, I was transferred to the tank corps. I still feel that those in charge thought I might be less dangerous to my companions and myself if I were surrounded by a steel tank.

I managed better there, but then someone took note of the fact that I was over six feet tall and that I was severely bouncing my head off the tank turret as we rolled merrily over those muddy Kentucky hills. Something had to be done because I was developing severe headaches as well as a number of swellings on my scalp. In the interest of serving my country I tried not to complain, but finally one of my sergeants brought the situation to the notice of the company commander.

To my relief, and I suspect to the relief of my commanding officers, I was called away from Fort Knox and assigned to a special group at the University of Kentucky called the Army Specialized Training Corps.

I have never fully understood the reason for the creation of the Army Specialized Training Corps. On the whole, the other members of the group seemed to me to be loners, not good with tools, inclined toward the academic life, and totally incapable in the use of firearms. I sometimes suspect that the Corps was created as a refuge for incompetent young men like me, to get us out of harm's way and at the same time to save the army the cost of damages we might unwittingly inflect on the war effort.

While traveling by train from Fort Knox to Lexington, I learned my seat companion was headed for the Army Specialized Training Corps, too. He was lost in reading a book and hardly grunted a greeting as I took the seat beside him.

The train had barely gotten underway when the

man emitted a shrill bleat-like scream. I was so shocked, as were the other soldiers around us, that I expected the MPs to arrive and place my seatmate in chains.

"My goat cry," he explained calmly, then returned to the book he had temporarily set aside. I was a remarkably unsophisticated young man. A short time at the University of Richmond had hardly gotten through the layers of poor schooling, backwoods prejudices, and almost no exposure to serious music or literature. I had read a bit, but it was unguided and consisted mainly of hit-and-miss discarded books sent to what we euphemistically called the Schuyler Library.

The GI sitting next to me on the train had a scowl on his face, which I was to learn was his way of hiding a sensitive and compassionate countenance. He had left his studies at Temple University and volunteered to serve in the Army. He was already having second thoughts.

"My name is Paul Nusnick," he said. "What's yours?"

I told him and asked what he was reading.

"Thomas Wolfe," he said. "Have you read him?"

I had to confess that I had not.

"Then you'd better get started," he said, and placed in my hands the book he had been reading, entitled *Look Homeward, Angel*. When I read the book I learned the origin of Nusnick's "goat cry." Wolfe wrote about such a cry that would come out of the depth of his being when he was deeply moved by an experience or a memory.

It was the beginning of a friendship with Paul Nusnick that would last till his death. When he learned that I was appallingly ignorant of serious music, at our next stop he led me to a music store where he played the pizzicato movement of Tchaikovsky's *Third Symphony*. The copy of *Look Homeward, Angel* was the beginning a lifelong love of everything that Thomas Wolfe has ever written.

From the very first I felt a kinship with another child of the hills who is destined to go far beyond the horizons, the prejudices, and the ignorance that hemmed him in during his growing up. While the circumstances and structure of our families were different, the feelings of kinship were very similar.

Even though Nusnick became my mentor, I think he was a little insane. At formations where our commanding officer would inspect his soldiers' posture, shoeshine, belt buckles, and general demeanor, Nusnick would stick out his stomach in a ridiculous and obvious attempt to satire the proper military posture.

Once, at inspection, our captain stopped in front of Nusnick and demanded, "What's wrong with you, soldier? You pregnant?"

"I could be, sir," Paul answered. "I've been screwed enough in this army!"

Wolfe's novel *You Can't Go Home Again* would continue to resonate throughout my life. I realized that Wolfe meant more than simply returning to a physical home, but also to innocence and youth and a less complicated world.

I became a serious reader of Wolfe's books, collecting modestly priced copies of most of them, and even visiting the home in Asheville, North Carolina, where he spent most of his growing years.

Many years later, when I had become a professional writer, I had a unique opportunity to come to know a great deal about Thomas Wolfe, the man.

I was a staff writer at NBC working on a radio show called *Biography in Sound*. It was a quality show. We chose a subject, usually a person of note, then interviewed as many people as we could find who had known or been associated with that person. We would then edit the tapes into a portrait of that person.

Upon beginning my association with the program, I quickly suggested Thomas Wolfe as a subject. The idea was approved and I was appointed to produce the segment.

Several people were still alive and willing to reminisce about Wolfe. Madeline Boyd, who had acted as his agent, was still alive and available. Another woman who had been his friend recorded her reminiscences. One of his editors, Edward Aswell, was a rich source of information, but it was his sister, Mabel

Wolfe Wheaton, who provided the richest and most revealing memories.

Almost all of Wolfe's writing was autobiographical. Sometimes he did not even bother to change the name of the real person he used as a model for a supposedly fictitious character. His mother, father, brothers, and his sister were easily recognizable as themselves in his writing.

I sat with Mabel in the studio and listened raptly as she spoke of their childhood. When she referred to characters as "Mama" or "Papa," their real life images came vividly to mind because I knew them from her brother's books.

The character of Helen in *Look Homeward, Angel* is easily recognizable as Mabel Wolfe Wheaton. To my near disbelief here I was, face to face with her, the real life sister of the writer I had come to revere.

She had a quality that I think many Southern women of her generation shared. It expressed itself in a kind of distancing, a reserve, a slight lack of trust with strangers — especially Northern strangers. But I think after she heard the documentary I produced about him she sensed and appreciated my deep admiration for her brother's work, and in time I recognized that she had accepted me as a friend.

She came to New York from her home in Raleigh from time to time in connection with her position as executor of her brother's estate. Frequently on these trips she would call me and we would have lunch.

Mabel Wheaton

Courtesy: Pack Memorial Library, Asheville, N.C.

On one of these occasions she promised that the next time she visited she was going to bring me an autographed copy of one of her brother's books.

Today an autographed copy of one of Thomas Wolfe's novels would bring from ten to fifteen thousand dollars. Even back then such a copy would have commanded a goodly sum.

I struggled with my conscience. Should I tell her

the real value of such a gift? I decided it would not be useful.

As she promised, the next time she came to New York she called me for lunch and presented me with one of her brother's books. It was a copy of *Of Time and the River*, and inscribed on the flyleaf was the autograph: "Presented to my friend, Earl Hamner Jr." It was signed: Mabel Wolfe Wheaton.

At that same lunch she asked me a curious question. "Are you a married man, Mr. Hamner?"

I told her that I was.

"Then I can tell you," she said, "that I have cancer of the reproductive organs." I recognized that for a woman of her background it would have been indelicate for her to reveal such information to an unmarried man.

Several months later I read that she had died.

THE GIFT OF ACHIEVEMENT
Belle Becker—Random House Editor

Ever since I made the decision that I was going to become a writer come hell or high water, I had been
keeping notes on a novel that was to be published as
Spencer's Mountain.

From time to time I had also been writing frag-
ments of another novel. It told the story of Althea
Peeler, a lonely backwoods girl who belonged to a religious group called the Holy Rollers.

A curious thing happened, and I have learned from
other writers that it is not unusual. The second book
suddenly developed acceleration. It had a life of its
own. It just kept going. I was so possessed by the people and the subject matter that when I sat down to
write, it was this book that seized my attention.

Very briefly, the book tells the story of the tragic
and comedic events that explode during a week in
which a charismatic preacher comes to town to conduct a religious revival.

I knew something about revivals. When I was a

129

youngster, itinerant preachers would hold daylong outdoor services broken only by "dinner on the ground," as the noon picnic was called.

These ministers were dramatists. They knew their audiences and they knew how to manipulate them.

Smoke fairly snorted from their nostrils. Hell and damnation became so real the heat was palpable. They would begin their sermons in soft, comforting, beguiling voices. And then the volume built steadily to a breathless terrifying, sobbing, volcanic exhortation to "Come to Jesus" and then climaxing with vivid images of the Hell that waited those of us who turned our backs on Him.

The signal that we had "Received the Call" was that Jesus touched us on the shoulder. I never received that healing touch and would leave the place in terror and foreboding of the fires of Hell, which was the best that could be in store for a sinner like me.

I wrote a great deal of *Fifty Roads to Town* at night. After fulfilling my duties to NBC during the day I would take a break, usually stopping at a bar called Hurley's that used to be on the corner of Sixth Avenue and 49th Street. Usually by the time I returned to my office everybody had left for the evening and I could settle down to privacy and an uninterrupted session of writing.

Some nights I would lose track of time. I would work so late that the passenger elevators would have been turned off and I would be obliged to take the freight elevator. I remember that the writing went so smoothly and I would become so intense that I was wound tight as a drum by the end of the night. And so by one and two in the morning I would slip into Jimmy Ryan's, a jazz joint, located at that time on 52nd Street. There I would have a beer and let the music help me unwind.

A friend read the manuscript that was partially handwritten, partially typed, and filled with insertions, revisions, and inked-out sections. In spite of the miserable typing job, my friend thought the book was extraordinary, even publishable. He had a friend at Random House, an editor, named Belle Becker.

I phoned her. She was cordial and invited me to stop by her office the following Friday.

I think she intended this to merely be a courtesy call, but I was determined to take my manuscript with me. Problem: It was unreadable in its rough state.

Then another Generous Woman came to my rescue. Her name was Patty Gabani Sauer. She also worked at NBC and was part of a circle of a few close friends. Patty learned of my predicament, organized a group of her friends, all excellent typists, and parceled out a chapter to each one. By Friday she returned my messy old manuscript to me along with a new one. The new one was beautifully typed on heavy bond paper. It was fresh and crisp and even some of my more imaginative attempts at spelling had been corrected.

In those days Random House was located in a stately old mansion at 457 Madison Avenue. Patty had boxed the manuscript in a neat stationery box, and I carried it as if it were filled with diamonds. I remember walking from my office past St. Patrick's Cathedral and silently asking, "Please God!" and then I bounded up to the second floor where Belle Becker's office was located.

The receptionist announced me and soon an attractive, short, bookish-looking woman appeared and invited me back to her office. The entire room was lined with books. There was some brief talk about my background and then she said, "Put your manuscript there on my desk."

There were several piles of manuscripts, and I placed mine on top of one pile, never knowing that I had made an excellent choice.

Miss Becker saw me back to the lobby and explained that she had mountains of manuscripts waiting to be read and weighed for their publication value. She went on to say that she read them in the order of their arrival and that it might be a while before she came to mine, and would I please be patient.

I promised I would.

On Monday my phone rang and Belle Becker explained that she always took a pile of manuscripts home with her for the weekend. By mistake she took a different pile than the one she was supposed to. My manuscript had been on the top of the pile, and she said that I had written a fine book, and subject to Bennett Cerf's approval, Random House would like to publish *Fifty Roads to Town*.

I walked out of my Rockefeller Center office, rushed over to the Random House building, trampling pedestrians, in a state of complete euphoria. I stood there and admired the home of "my publisher," and if someone passing by heard a strange, guttural cry of utter happiness they might have heard my version of Thomas Wolfe's "goat cry!"

I was numb with shock for several days, then elation set in, and finally belief, and eventually I did what Belle Becker had instructed me to do. She said that often a newly published writer will get so carried away with acceptance that he or she spends valuable time in boasting, preening, and showing off. She said the wisest thing I could do would be to start a new book. I had already done considerable work on *Spencer's Mountain* and so I got right back to work.

During the course of editing the book, Belle and I would meet from time to time. We became good friends. She was married to Abner Sideman, an editor at *Look* magazine and I was often invited to their apartment on West 12th Street.

As we worked together Belle asked where I had

found the three lines of poetry on page 223 and if I had gotten permission to use them. I explained that they came from a poem by Muriel Rukeyser called "Effort at Speech Between Two People." I also told her that the poem was one of my favorites and I had found it in a volume titled *War Department Education Manual EM 131, Modern American Poetry* edited by Louis Untermeyer. I just checked the title because I still have the book, a dog-eared, shabby old thing. The back jacket is missing and it shows signs of wear seldom seen in a book of poetry. I found the book in a USO in Louisville while stationed at Fort Knox and had carried it with me all through World War II.

Belle was not acquainted with the poet, but she was familiar with her work.

"Where do you start tracking down somebody like that?" I asked.

"You'd be surprised whom you'll find in the Manhattan phone book," she said.

I looked up the name Muriel Rukeyser in the phone book. I was astonished to learn that she lived only four blocks from my apartment. When I told her why I was calling she promptly gave me permission to quote from her poem.

Belle was also helpful in my getting my first agent. She told me that contracts for most first-time novelists are fairly standard and that my advance would not be extravagant, but that she had a friend who would get the best contract Random might give a first-time author. And so she sent me to see Bernice Baumgarten.

Bernice was one of the agents at a literary agency called Brandt and Brandt. She was a genteel and rather aristocratic woman who lived out in Bucks County, Pennsylvania, and commuted to her New York office.

Bernice's office was furnished in disarmingly comfortable traditional furniture. We sat in rocking chairs while we talked. Belle had already sent her a copy of

Bernice Baumgarten

Fifty Roads to Town and Bernice admired the book tremendously. This was an extra thrill for me because I had learned that Bernice was married to James Gould Cozzens, the author of *By Love Possessed*, and certainly had the highest standards.

On one visit to Random House I saw a striking-looking gentleman sitting across from me in the waiting room. When I recognized he was William Faulkner I successfully restrained myself from going over and announcing that I was a Random House writer, too. After a moment his editor, Saxe Cummings, came into the lobby and they left for lunch.

I went swooning into Belle's office and told her I had seen Faulkner. "He's here doing some revisions," said Belle. "His favorite restaurant is just down the street. Has lunch there every day."

I found out that Faulkner's favorite restaurant was Le Marmiton on 53rd. Whenever I found out he was in town I would go there, order my own lunch and then watch the great man eat. Mostly he drank.

Suddenly I had entered a charmed circle. I was a published writer! I had been published by an esteemed publisher. Still, I had no idea what lofty company I had been keeping until years later when I received a call from Bernice. She was calling to say that she was retiring, but that she would continue to represent just one author.

"I hope it's me," I said.

"No," she said. "It's Winston Churchill."

Belle Becker and I were to become neighbors as well as colleagues when Jane and I moved to 44 West 12th Street. Belle and Abner lived directly across the street, so we continued our friendship until Jane and I moved to California.

It was a special pleasure in a *Waltons* episode, in which John-Boy has his first book published, to give his editor the name Belle Becker. I let her know in advance when the episode would be aired. She had retired by then and was genuinely moved. In a thank-you note she said it was the greatest tribute she had ever received from one of her writers.

I have had many books published since that time, but never has the experience been so happy as that first one was thanks to the generosity of Patty Gabani Sauer, Belle Becker, and Bernice Baumgarten.

THE GIFT OF VALIDATION

Harper Lee—Novelist

When I speak to students of writing, one piece of advice I try to instill in them, if nothing else, is a single idea: Write what you care for. Write what you are passionate about!

When I first started writing I did not know exactly where my passion lay, but over the years it has proved to be the family I was born into, my ancestors and our history, our home and the small town of Schuyler, Virginia, where I was born. I felt a keen and abiding kinship with my hometown. I felt bonded to my ancestral earth. Place is where writers and writing spring from. We feel a kinship with that earth that sustains and nurtures us, whether it be the red Virginia clay or the grass plains of the Midwest or the rich loam of the Mississippi Delta.

While I did not have a central story, over the years I found myself almost without knowing why, writing down memories of growing up, thoughts about the people I had known, faces and voices I had known back in the foothills of the Blue Ridge Mountains.

I can remember sitting in a pup tent in the hedgerows of Normandy writing while bombers flew overhead toward Berlin and the light of day faded, and remembering the sights and sounds that were part of our lives during the Great Depression, when I was a boy.

I had always felt that no one had enjoyed quite so good a life until I arrived in New York City many years later and was told I had come from a deprived society and that my people had been afflicted with a disease that the sociologists called "familism." They defined familism as a social disorder in which the family is considered more important than the individual. Even after I discovered that I suffered from "familism" I was not convinced. I just thought we loved one another.

The discovery, too, that I had been raised in a depressed area and in deprived conditions did not deter me from the knowledge that I had been lucky to be born into my family, and rather than feeling depression I remembered my early years to be the most joyful of times.

There was a dream my father had, a promise he made to my mother. He told it many times. In those days when there was little else to sustain us his dream gave us hope and sustenance. His dream was somehow the key that unlocked the traditional values our family stood for and became the fountainhead of my writing.

"Up on the mountain," he would say, "I am going to build a house for your mama and you children. It's going to be painted white with green trim, because that's your mama's favorite color. I'm going to put a long porch along the front where we can all sit of an evening, and in the living room there's going to be what they call a picture window where we can look out and watch the dogwood come out in the spring time and the trees turn all their colors in the fall."

There came a time when, in the words of Katherine Anne Porter, the book told me it had cooked enough and the time had come to start writing.

I set about writing a semi-autobiographical novel that was to become my second book, *Spencer's Mountain*.

A year or so earlier the publishing world had witnessed the appearance of a classic: *To Kill a Mockingbird* by a previously unknown writer named Harper Lee. It was a landmark book. In time it was turned into a noble film and remains one of the finest pieces of writing of the twentieth century.

My editor, Jim Silberman, sent a completed copy of the manuscript to Miss Lee and in response she wrote an endorsement that gave the book enough of a push to send it straight to the top of the best-seller lists.

"Thank you," she wrote in her letter to my editor. "And thank you again for beating me over the head with *Spencer's Mountain*. At first glance, I must confess to a sinking feeling that Mr. Hamner might be another sheep in Wolfe's clothing. He is nothing of the kind. His gifts are strictly his own, and he is richly endowed.

"It is so easy to create a villain or an eccentric. It is so hard to create good people and make them unforgettable. Each character in *Spencer's Mountain* is memorable because life itself flows in abundance from each. One finds pure joy in reading, for a change, a positive statement on the potentialities of man."

The endorsement continues in that vein and ends with this final sentence:

"He is a fine writer, and he must be a fine man." Such an endorsement from such a distinguished writer demands attention, and I believe it was largely due to her praise that the book became a bestseller and subsequently a popular motion picture starring Henry Fonda, Maureen O'Hara, and James McArthur.

Such a positive endorsement also carried with it the responsibility of becoming the best writer I could be. I have tried to live up to that faith in me.

When Jim Person finished writing my biography, *Earl Hamner: From Walton's Mountain to Tomorrow*, he sent the manuscript to Harper Lee and asked for a comment. Once again she proved to be a good friend and supporter and the book jacket of the bio proudly carried these words: "Since *Spencer's Mountain* I have followed Earl Hamner's career with much interest and much satisfaction, having picked a winner!" That's the equivalent of knocking a home run and having Babe Ruth say, "Nice hit."

I never met Harper Lee in person but we spoke briefly by telephone while she was in Hollywood during the filming of *To Kill a Mockingbird*.

She was leaving the next day and I had the feeling that she could hardly wait to get out of Hollywood and return home to Alabama.

As far as most of us know she has never written another book, but it remains my dream that someday another "great American novel" by Harper Lee will appear. However, if that does not happen we have no grounds for complaint. She has already conquered Everest. There is no need to go there again.

Whenever I publish a book I send her a copy, and I will send this one to her, as always, with my enduring affection, admiration, and gratitude.

THE GIFT OF PATIENCE
Eleanor Roosevelt—Herself

I was late! I was late! I was horrifyingly late, and waiting for me in a recording studio at NBC was one of the most famous and widely respected ladies in the world, the wife of a former president of the United States, the first lady of the land, Mrs. Eleanor Roosevelt!

At the time I was writing and producing a radio series called *Biography in Sound*. The series featured the taped commentaries of people who had known or been associated with a notable person. Great numbers of tapes were recorded and then assembled in a chronology that would fit into an hour. We produced biographies of such people as Scott Fitzgerald, Thomas Wolfe, Robert Benchley, and Teddy Roosevelt, whose biography I was preparing at that time.

Eleanor Roosevelt had consented to arrange her busy schedule so she could stop by Rockefeller Plaza and record her memories of her "Uncle Teddy."

At the appointed time I was hopelessly stuck

Eleanor Roosevelt

downtown in a stalled subway train realizing there was no way to make the appointment. Finally my train began to move again and brought me to Rockefeller Center. I rushed into the studio forty minutes late, only to find Mrs. Roosevelt patiently waiting.

I started to apologize, but she stopped me and said, "Please, you gave me time to catch up on some letters!"

What a gracious thing for a great lady to say to a

fledgling writer. It was as if I had done her a great favor. That I had imposed on her time was totally overlooked, and by turning it around she transformed my guilt into energy that resulted in a rich and productive interview. The event also taught me that every moment in life is precious and should be utilized. Time is not to kill, but to use.

One of the stories Mrs. Roosevelt told me that day was of "Uncle Teddy" and his theory that the best way to teach someone to swim was simply to throw them in the water. She said, "I was just a little girl visiting my uncle out at Oyster Bay. He threw me off the end of the dock. I promptly disproved his theory, sank to the bottom of the bay, and had to be rescued!"

THE GIFT OF FUN

Tallulah Bankhead—Actress

Being on the writing staff at NBC was something like working on the "flying squad" in a department store. If there is a run on gloves, a clerk from the flying squad rushes to the glove counter. If a long line forms in the toy department additional clerks are assigned there.

I liked being on the NBC flying squad. It meant a variety of assignments in different departments. I met people I might otherwise never have known, and I learned a great deal about the broadcast business. It also provided an occasion for me to meet one of the most fascinating people of that day and time.

Tallulah Bankhead has been described as outrageous, outspoken, brilliant, bawdy, profane, impetuous, notorious, driven, tragic, hedonistic, lonely, unstoppable, superstitious, ravishing, infuriating, and classy. And that's just a few descriptions from the jacket of Denis Brian's biography *Tallulah, Darling*. As Brian notes: "An encounter with Tallulah was unforgettable." I can attest to the truth of that statement.

Tallulah Bankhead was born January 31, 1902 in Huntsville, Alabama, and named after her grandmother who had been named after a waterfall in Georgia. The Bankheads were a prominent political family. Her father was a United States Representative and Speaker of the House. Tallulah loved him without reservation.

As a child Tallulah seems to have shown every indication of the adult she would become: a mercurial, engaging little girl who constantly sought attention by singing, reciting poetry, and when all else failed, turning cartwheels.

She arrived in New York as a headstrong sixteen-year-old girl of arresting beauty. She was immediately adopted by theatrical folk and for one so young was right at home in such heady company as the writers and artists who gathered at the Algonquin Round Table.

There is not much to show of her work today. She performed most of her work on stage and radio. There is one movie, *Lifeboat*, which is worth watching if it ever comes available on DVD.

While assigned to the flying squad of the writing department, I was occasionally given an assignment in the obituary department. One of the first obits I was assigned to write was radio legend Fred Allen's. The executive in charge supplied me with the telephone of

Tallulah Bankhead

Allen's widow, named Portland, and instructed me to call her and ask for a statement. I could not bring myself to intrude on the lady at such a painful time and I refused to do it. My supervisor, Van Woodward, interceded and I kept my job, but I was in disfavor with that particular executive for a good many years.

When Lionel Barrymore died I was assigned to write his obituary. Rather than write a tribute specifically to Lionel Barrymore, I wrote a celebration of all actors. It was a little bit corny, but it expressed my sincere admiration and appreciation of actors and the gifts they bring to us. I remember that the obituary I wrote said, in part, that actors are a separate race of people, that they come alive at eight-thirty when the curtain goes up, and that when they die they go not to Heaven, but to The Theater.

Miss Bankhead had been a friend of the whole Barrymore family, but most especially of Lionel, and she agreed to record a tribute to him for broadcast over NBC radio.

The director for this particular segment was a nice guy named George Voutsas, a courteous, capable, easy-going guy I had worked with often. George insisted I go with him to Tallulah's apartment to make the recording. I was more than willing.

I had seen Tallulah once on stage in Noel Coward's *Private Lives*. The prospect of meeting her in person could not have been more thrilling.

In those days Tallulah was living at the Elysée Hotel, in an apartment that was later rented by Tennessee Williams. Tallulah's friend and companion at the time was actress/comedian Patsy Kelly.

On the appointed morning at eleven o'clock George Voutsas and I phoned from the hotel lobby, were given the number of Tallulah's apartment, and were told to come on up. Patsy greeted us at the door, ushered us into the living room, and said, "Miss B's not up yet, but I'll go see what I can do."

She disappeared down the hallway.

From a room somewhere deep in the apartment came the muffled sounds of coughs, groans, curses, and lamentations. Patsy returned after a while and said, "She'll be along."

While we were waiting the engineer set up his microphone and recording equipment, and after not too long a time something between a gargle and a groan was heard approaching. It was the signal that Tallulah was about to enter.

At first she simply materialized. Then she paused and placed one hand high on the doorframe in a self-mocking gesture which seemed to say "This is how I am expected to enter!" She had combed her hair, put on some lipstick, and she was dressed in a pink satin robe. She was barefooted. I had heard that wearing clothes was abhorrent to Miss B. I thought that it maybe was a concession to strangers that she had dressed at all.

No one spoke for a moment until Tallulah said in a hollow voice, "Champagne!"

"For everybody, Miss B?" asked Patsy.

"Just for me, dahling," replied Tallulah.

George and I introduced ourselves. Tallulah acknowledged us with a sweet smile, muttered something about laryngitis, then settled on a sofa while she read the script and waited for the champagne.

It was a quick read. Afterward she turned to George and said, "This is beautiful. Who wrote it?"

George pointed to me, and said, "Earl, Miss B, another Southerner."

"Naturally, dahling," said Tallulah and gave me a smile I would never forget. The rest of the recording session went like a dream.

Tallulah was doing her radio show called *The Big Show* for NBC in those days. For the declining days of live radio her show was quite special. Her guest stars alone comprised a list of who's who of the theatrical world. Her musical director was Meredith Wilson, the composer of *The Music Man*. Because of her husky voice and his supposed naivety (he was from Iowa, so wrongfully presented as the home of rubes), he would address her as "Miss Bankhead, sir."

There was always a pretend situation in which Tallulah would find herself put to a test of some kind. I remember one radio broadcast in which her limo ran out of gas and she had to take the subway. As she entered the subway she politely asked directions to "First Class."

At NBC I would run into her from time to time and she would always ask about my writing. Sometimes she would ask about news about a pompous gentleman we both knew.

I told her that I had heard that he was going into the hospital for an operation.

"I know, dahling," she said. "He won't say what it is for but he's so damn serious about it I suspect it's a brain tumor."

When I learned that the operation was for hemorrhoids I told her, and she said, "Well, dahling, it was on his brain after all!"

And then she laughed that husky whiskey bray and warned me never to repeat what she had said.

Many years later I was able to sell my script "Appalachian Autumn" to the *CBS Playhouse*. A gifted woman named Barbara Schultz was producer, and Martin Manullis, one of the pioneers in the Golden Age of television, was executive producer. My script told the story of a young Appalachian boy, a talented potter living in the exhausted coal fields of Virginia. A young domestic Peace Corps worker, he believes he will lead the community out of poverty.

We assembled a formidable cast. Arthur Kennedy played the father and Teresa Wright came out from New York to play the mother. When the suggestion that Estelle Winwood would be perfect for the role of the steely old grandmother, I could not have agreed more quickly. I was well aware that Miss Winwood had been a long-time friend of Tallulah's and I selfishly I wanted to get to work with her.

Miss Winwood was getting along in years, but she was prompt for rehearsals, and appeared on time when we began filming. And she knew her lines. One of her secretaries, one of a series of good-looking young men, would deliver her to the studio, escort her from the dressing room to the stage, and see that she got home.

And she played her role to perfection. I am aware of a certain cadence, a use of certain words and rhythms that are holdovers in Appalachian speech that were in use in England centuries ago. It was interesting to hear language of today that had evolved from what had been used in Chaucer's day spoken by an accomplished English actress.

What was even more fun was to visit with Miss Winwood and listen to Tallulah stories.

"Is it true that she would take off her clothes sometimes?" I asked.

"At the drop of a tuppence," said Miss Winwood.

The last time I saw Miss Winwood she was coming out of a restaurant in Sherman Oaks, California. She was being escorted by a "secretary" on either side and all signs pointed to the fact that they had not been to a temperance meeting.

"We've been celebrating my birthday," she said, listing just a little toward one of the secretaries.

"Do you tell how old you are?" I asked.

"My dear," she said in a very grand manner, "we are one hundred years of age."

"Happy Birthday," I said. "Are you still working in films?"

"No, dahling," she answered. "They won't hire me anymore. I cawn't remember my lines."

A limo arrived just then. The secretaries helped her enter and they drove away.

THE GIFT OF KINDNESS
Kay Thompson—Personality

One of my assignments when I was on the writing staff at NBC was to write continuity for *The Andy Williams Show*. This was not one of the expensive spectacular Andy Williams Christmas shows we were to see at the top of his career, later on television. This was early in his career. This show was on radio, and Andy alternated the time slot three days a week with singer Helen O'Connell.

Working with Andy was a pleasure. He had his own vision of how he wanted to present himself and felt free to change the dialogue to fit his "style."

Off screen he was as genial and as charming as on-screen. And that voice! It has been described as champagne honey, gold and silver, but without question it is smooth and romantic and unique.

Andy, as a boy, had been the youngest member of the Williams Brothers, a group composed of Andy's own brothers from Clear Lake, Iowa. For many years they worked as backup for entertainer and nightclub singer Kay Thompson.

Kay Thompson continued to star as a singer, but she also became a writer. Her creation of *Eloise*, the little girl who lived at the Plaza, became an international success and added more luster to the already prestigious Plaza Hotel in New York.

At least once during the frigid New York winters I would acquire a germ that would attack my respiratory system. A common cold could lay me low for a week. God forbid if pneumonia took hold.

During one of my bouts with a respiratory ailment, I was confined to bed for a week. I phoned Andy to let him know that I was sick and that another writer was assigned to write his show temporarily.

In the course of working with Andy, he had learned two things about me. One, that I had lived in Paris and still loved the city. Second, that I had read and loved Kay Thompson's *Eloise*.

My telephone rang. The voice over the phone was husky and seductive.

"This is Kay Thompson," she said. "Andy tells me you are not feeling well, so I thought you might like to hear my new book."

I was astonished and even more so when Miss Thompson proceeded to read the entire text of *Eloise in Paris*.

It was a truly unforgettable experience. I was never to meet her in person, but I think of her whenever Jane and I are in New York, for there is always an obligatory visit to the Plaza's Palm Court and to the portrait of Eloise in a prominent position in the lobby.

I saw Andy not long ago. I was in Missouri to give a speech at Southwest Missouri University. My hosts treated Jane and me to a trip to Branson, where Andy Williams has his own theater. Knowing that Andy and I had worked together they had arranged a visit. Andy was most gracious and introduced me from the audience to the other guests.

It was thoughtful of him, and the pleasure of hearing applause was a new and intoxicating experience. Actors hear it all the time, but it is rare for a writer to receive such adulation.

Applause is addictive. I can hardly wait to get back to Branson, and when I go I will take every means to let Andy know that I am in his audience.

THE GIFT OF STYLE

Patricia Neal—Actress

In her autobiography *As I Am* Patricia Neal writes, "While we were in New York I received my first Hollywood job offer since *The Subject Was Roses*. Fielder Cook, the director, sent me a script called *The Homecoming*. It was for television, a Christmas story about a rural Virginia family during the Depression. It was perfect for me."

The project was also perfect for Fielder Cook. Fielder had been one of the pioneers in what has come to be known as the Golden Age of television. Those were the days of live television drama that spawned such fine writers as Reginald Rose, Ernest Kinoy, Tad Mosel, and Rod Serling. I had not met Fielder, but I knew his work, and I was also aware that he was a Virginian. A tall, stately man, Fielder was an arresting figure. He habitually wore an ice cream suit and a planter's hat that was somehow suggestive of both the rural and the urbane at the same time.

Fielder and I became friends immediately. He came from a Waynesboro family and knew the area I wrote about. We would often have lunch together. When he walked into a restaurant, even in the company of a well-known actress, every eye followed him rather than his companion. The only exception was when he walked into a restaurant with Patricia Neal. It was not something she willed. It simply happened. She was a star and she commanded a star's right: undivided adoration.

Patricia was living in Great Missenden, a small town outside of London at the time with her husband, Raold Dahl. She arrived in Los Angeles having memorized every word of the script.

She asked for only one change. I had named the mother Dorrie after my own mother whose name was Doris. Patricia asked if the name could be changed to Olivia after the daughter the Dahls had lost as a result of a rare complication of measles encephalitis. Of course I gladly made the change.

"I found it surprisingly easy to slip back into southern speech patterns," she writes. "It helped, of course, that I was surrounded by unreconstructed southerners on the set. Fielder has lived in Georgia. Earl is a Virginian. And one of my costars, Edgar Bergen, claimed his parents had emigrated from 'southern' Sweden."

It was not just her Southern background that made

Patricia Neal

her so unforgettable as Olivia. Patricia has a quality that is hard to describe. Sexy, beautiful, appealing, glamorous, lustrous. Hollywood has a wealth of ladies who have such qualities, but Patricia has something in addition.

Patricia possessed a quality that made her stand out above all the others. Her enormous strength, the image of "the earth mother," made for perfect casting for the leading role in Bertolt Brecht's classic *Mother Courage*. Her voice says it all. It has been described as "a mighty Wurlitzer of a voice" but it is indicative of who Patricia Neal really is.

Filming of *The Homecoming* proceeded without mishap. The interior scenes were shot in a studio on Radford Avenue in Studio City. The cast melded together, became a family, believable, and almost heartbreakingly reminiscent of the family I had left behind in Virginia. For her part, Patricia brought incredible strength to the character of the mother.

The Homecoming went on the air a few days before Christmas Eve of 1971. The reception was gratifying. Both the audience and the critics loved the show. Someone else also loved the show, somebody very powerful, William Paley, the Chairman of the Board of CBS. Mr. Paley not only liked it but suggested it had the makings of a series.

When we were given the go ahead to film a television series Patricia's name came up but the casting agents felt her status as a movie star was undiminished, and her health might be a question, and she would have no interest in doing a series. They were wrong.

In *As I Am* she writes: "I received an Emmy nomination for my Olivia Walton but lost to Glenda Jackson, a lady whom I had never met. The show continued, of course, as the long running series *The Waltons*. Why didn't I do the series? Simple. No one asked me."

Soon after the series went on the air Richard Thomas and I had lunch with Patricia in the dining room at Warner Studio. One of the first things she asked was, "Who is that woman who is doing my part?" I am happy to say that she and "that woman," Michael Learned, worked together later and became fast friends.

Some years after we had worked together I met Patricia for lunch and mentioned that I was going to the airport to meet my mother.

"I want to meet her," Patricia said.

Patricia was due to leave the following day for Vancouver, where she was to start work on a film. Instead, she phoned the production company and asked them to change her flight to the following day. She then phoned me and said, "Would your mother have tea with me tomorrow afternoon at the Beverly Wilshire?"

I escorted my mother to the door of Patricia's hotel room. Pat opened the door and said, "Shoo. Your mother and I don't need you. Come back later."

I came back for my mother two hours later. I was curious. Patricia was a woman of the world, a sophisticated movie star of international acclaim, and the former wife of a best-selling author.

My mother, while a lady in her own right, had not traveled. She had only a high school education and had spent most of her life washing clothes, cooking three meals a day, and cleaning for an enormous family.

What did these two women have in common, I wondered?

"What did you and Patricia talk about?" I asked my mother.

"Oh, lots of things," she said, "I told her all about Schuyler and she told me all about Hollywood."

THE GIFT OF
UNDERSTANDING

Michael Learned—Actress

In addition to her sympathetic and multidimensional portrayal of Olivia Walton, a role inspired by my own mother, I owe Michael Learned a second debt of gratitude. It came about in a curious way. It was not Michael's intention that day to bestow a gift on me or anybody else. Gift giving was the last thing in her mind. By signing on to do a series she had become trapped in an extremely frustrating situation. She was at the mercy of production executives, writers, directors, publicity people, network executives, business managers, agents, schedules, and she wanted to take back her life. She was mad as hell. She was out to change her life, but what it led to changed *my* life in a dramatic and positive way.

I should point out that anger is about the last emotion I would ordinarily associate with Michael. In person she is gracious, sensitive, loving, intelligent, kind, and thoughtful. She is so beautiful that on television

Michael Learned

we had to costume her in the plainest outfits we could find in order to make her beauty believable. Even dressing her in shabby Depression-era clothing we could not diminish her beauty.

To cast Michael as Olivia Walton was a coup. At the time she was a member of the distinguished San Francisco acting group known as the American Repertory Theater. Its members were classic actors, expert especially in the work of Shakespeare.

Patricia Neal had played the Olivia role in an earlier version. Our casting people had already decided that Pat's career was so established in movies that she would not even consider an offer to do television. They were wrong as it turned out. Pat would have been interested, but nobody approached her! So the search was on.

Michael happened to be in Los Angeles, and her agent persuaded her to do a screen test for the role of Olivia. Michael did the test almost as a lark. Our production team was floored when we saw the screen test and became even more in love when we met Michael in person. She was then, and remains today, a radiant actress, an exciting and loyal friend.

A contract was arranged and Michael joined the cast of talented people we had already assembled. Physically and temperamentally, she belonged immediately.

In series television if you make one mistake you are doomed. If the music is wrong, you are going down the tubes. If the script doesn't work, goodbye series. If one of the actors doesn't fit with the rest of the cast, there is no hope. On *The Waltons* every element was perfect and fit together like the pieces of a Chinese puzzle. Most especially the cast members were talented actors, attractive, dedicated people, and the happy mixture of all the elements led to the legendary success of the series. More than thirty-five years later it is still in reruns around the world. I can always tell where it is being seen from the fan mail I receive. Recently I have begun receiving mail from Calcutta! It is a special pleasure to me that the series is being discovered here at home by a whole new audience of young people who missed it the first time round.

To understand Michael's "gift" to me you need to spend an average day on the set of a hit television series. The "show-biz" aura of glamour and excitement quickly wears off and is replaced with the numbing knowledge that one is trapped in a contract that could last from five to ten years.

But it's a living and the money is reasonably good. For the leading lady in a long-running television series such as *The Waltons* the routine goes something as follows:

At five each morning you obey the alarm clock's bidding and tear yourself out of bed. You dress, grab a quick breakfast, risk your life driving in the brutal Los Angeles morning traffic and arrive at the studio by seven o'clock. Other sleepy actors are shuffling about and because you either love them or have to act with them for the day you try to be civil. The coffee at the Craft Service table is usually good. And that helps. There are all sorts of other healthy foods available but it's hard to turn down the comfort of a doughnut at that time of day. So you eat the damn thing and plan to jog to Santa Barbara later in the afternoon.

Finally, it is your turn in the makeup trailer. The

make-up artist is a sweet girl or guy and he or she has learned to know your moods, knows whether you want to be silent or to talk and is sympathetic. The actor in the next chair is babbling away on a phone. Captive to his inane conversation, you plan to cut his heart out at the first opportunity. You suffer through the hairdo, the lip gloss, eyebrows, cheeks, eyelashes, and finally the pancake makeup covering the entire face and any other exposed skin.

Next you're off to your dressing room where the costume person may or may not be waiting with your costume for the day. It's been fitted the night before, so all you have to do is get into it being careful to shake out any pins or needles inadvertently left over from a hastily tailored costume. It smells of cleaning fluid and somebody else's sweat.

An assistant knocks at the door to announce that you have five minutes to rehearsal. You look for your shoes while studying the script for the dialogue you'll have to deliver in the scene you're about to rehearse. You finally remember you left the shoes in your car, so a gofer is dispatched to the parking lot, and finally shoes, dialogue, makeup, costume, and actor skid onto the set. All the other actors have been waiting and try not to show their annoyance that you are late.

Finally it's time for the camera to roll when a phone call comes from home. It's the housekeeper informing you that someone left the front gate open and the beloved family dog has gone missing and is probably wandering loose around Beverly Hills. You ask the director if he can do the scene without you. He's sorry but unable to do as you ask. You steel yourself and report to the set, but there is a wait because one of the producers, at the last minute, has decided that the set is not right and has to be revised. You call home to find that the dog is not loose but has been discovered hiding under a bed. You realize you have been grinding your teeth and a migraine has set in.

The set having now been approved by several producers, the art director, and the director and the writer is now ready, and the cast reassembles. The scene to be filmed involves eleven actors (mother, father, grandmother, grandfather, and a herd of children) and it all takes place in the kitchen while the cast is at breakfast. The first take is easy enough: The mother makes her way from stove to table with a coffee pot in her hand. Reaching the table she smiles to her husband and says the one line she has been given in a six-page scene:

"Coffee?"

In the first take the director is not happy with the way one of the actors has delivered his line and asks for a second take. In the second take the actor reaches the questionable line, becomes self-conscious, breaks up, then starts to giggle. Other actors giggle in sympathy. The director delivers a short sermon on professionalism and then says, "Let's try it again!"

The actress playing the mother goes to the stove, picks up the coffee pot. The director calls "Camera" and the cameraman replies "Rolling!" "Action," calls the director. The leading lady starts for the table, wrinkles her face into the scripted smile, and then the director calls, "Cut!"

"What's the matter?" asks one of the actors.

"You're supposed to be eating breakfast," the director answers. "How come nobody's eating?"

"The food's gotten cold!" they shout in unison.

"Eat it anyway," orders the director. "We've got a schedule to make here!"

Time is called out while the chaperone of one of the child actors threatens to report the company to the union for serving inappropriate food to the actors. The actress playing the mother takes the coffee pot back to the stove and waits for the discussion to be resolved.

The prop man takes the cold plates from the table and replaces them with plates of warm food from the kitchen. Often a meal scene is so challenging and there are so many retakes that the actors rebel and food fights ensue. Cold mashed potatoes are rinsed out of more than one actor's hair at the end of the day.

The scene is just about to be filmed to everybody's satisfaction. The actors have all remembered their lines, the camera moved in and out and around the

way the director wanted it to, and everybody is looking forward to getting the next scene out of the way
when a loud voice is heard from the entrance to the
sound stage. It's a tour guide delivering his spiel to a
group of tourists, and the entire scene has to be shot
again.

And it's only nine o'clock in the morning!

The rest of the day appears just as stressful. There
is lunch with some reporter from Abyssinia representing the powerful Foreign Press Association, and a
photo shoot in Franklin Canyon when filming is finished. Home possibly around eight or nine o'clock
with an early call tomorrow!

Under the demands of repeating such a schedule
day after day, month after month, year after year, a
mountain of stress accumulates. It finally reaches a
point where it simply spills over.

Under somewhat similar circumstances after
months and then years of it, my friend Michael
reached the end of her rope.

I learned what stress had driven her to one afternoon when I received a call from one of my fellow
producers asking me to stop by his office. There he
showed me a copy of the script being filmed that day.

Whole lines of dialogue had been obliterated with
a heavy black marker. The script was wrinkled and
dog-eared as if it had been twisted in anger and
thrown across the room. I opened it to find such notes

as: "Six pages with only one line of dialogue!" "The character would not talk like this." "This is drivel and this is a stupid script." It was Michael's script.

And then *I* snapped! Nothing was more sacred to me in my work than The Script. Without the words, actors would have nothing to say. Without the words, directors would have nothing to direct. Everything depends on The Script. I was so dedicated to The Script that I insisted it be perfect in everything from content to appearance.

I, too, had been under pressure. The daily schedule of trips to the set, conferences with directors, budget meetings, script sessions with writers for future episodes, watching dailies, and attending casting sessions totally consumed every hour of the day. In between these duties I had waged a successful war with the network to keep the scripts true to my vision of the series. There was the added stress of insisting that characters based on my own family members were true to the real person. To make matters worse, I had neglected my own wife and children, skipped meals with them, arrived home late at night after putting the script to bed instead of putting my children to bed, and I was filled with guilt.

"What do you make of this?" asked the other producer, indicating Michael's script.

"I'm going to kill her!" I replied.

When I confronted Michael with my mutilated

script she was aghast.

"You weren't supposed to see that," she apologized. "I am trying to negotiate some changes in my contract, and I was using everything I could think of."

"Why didn't you come to me?"

"It had nothing to do with you! You weren't even supposed to see that. The scripts are fine."

But the damage was done. In truth, such little skirmishes between actors and producers take place all the time. The experience is supposed to roll off your back. The hard feelings simply dissolve and it's a friendly wave or a kiss on the cheek the next time your paths cross.

I wasn't up to such a sensible reaction. In a blind rage I went back to my office, packed all my personal belongings, and called Jane to say that I was quitting the job. I had had it with actors! I had had it with the production company! I had had it with television!

Jane listened thoughtfully and let me rave on. Finally, when I had unloaded much of my frustration, she said, "I think you need to talk with someone. Why not call that shrink our friends have mentioned?"

"I'm not crazy," I howled. "I don't need to see any shrink!"

That doctor was kind enough to see me later that day.

Ten years later I emerged a changed man. Very early I learned that it was not Michael that I was angry with. It was not even anger I was experiencing. It was rampant rage! It was rage so consuming that it was eating at my guts and my heart and my brain.

I liked Dr. Natterson on sight, and I also liked a framed quotation on his wall that read:

> The tiger eating at your heart,
> Let him out.
> Once freed he will
> Be no more fierce
> Than a child's rag doll,
> His ruthless claws a dream —
> All gone.

The first thing I discovered was that my anger with Michael was the smallest of my worries. Without being aware of it I was enraged, terrified, and filled with guilt and grief for reasons I did not understand.

Together Dr. Natterson and I discovered wounds, hurts so intolerable and a childhood tragedy so shocking that they had not just shadowed my life, but determined the course of every minute of every day of my life.

And under Natterson's guidance those wounds became, in the words of the plaque on his wall, "no more fierce than a child's rag doll."

You probably wonder what my relationship with Michael is like today. We are better friends than we were in those early years. Today with Michael, as with everyone else in my life, I am a better person.

No one is ever totally cleansed of deep psychic wounds. But I know now where my terror and grief and guilt came from, and I know how to deal with them. I am able to be a real friend to my family and to my friends, more trusting, more open, more honest, and more truly loving.

THE GIFT OF COURAGE

Ellen Corby—Actress

Ellen Corby was a generous person. She was especially generous in her contribution to *The Waltons*. Her generous gift to me was her interpretation of the role and her performance of Grandma Walton. In time we were to become good friends, but in the beginning we started off on the wrong foot.

Ellen and I first met at a reading of the script of *The Homecoming*. Usually I meet with actors prior to a final decision on casting, but Fielder Cook, the director, had suggested we cast her. I knew her work and agreed that she would make a fine "Grandma Walton."

At the initial read-through of the script I began to have misgivings. My own Grandmother Hamner had been a remarkably sweet-natured woman. Ellen was, in Hollywood terms, giving the character "an edge," making her sharp at times, in no way reminiscent of the real woman. Following the reading I asked Ellen to stop by my office so we could discuss her character.

She came and was most gracious until I launched into my vision of Grandma Walton.

"My own grandmother was a sweet little woman," I began. "She always wore a sprig of forget-me-not in her hair and she had a little parakeet named Bird that used to sit on her finger and. . . ."

But Ellen was ahead of me, knew what I was going to say, and interrupted.

"Young man," she said, "You have got so many sweet people in this show that the audience is going to die of sugar diabetes."

How dare this arrogant old woman talk to me this way, I thought. I am the writer and producer of this thing. We are talking about my grandmother! How dare she!

"I'll give you sweetness if the script calls for it and I feel it is dramatically right for the moment," she went on. "But I will also give you tartness. In all these oranges, I'll be the lemon."

I was a little miffed when she breezed out of the office, but as time went by—especially when the special became a series—I recognized the wisdom of Ellen's choice. When everybody else was easily led into one scheme or another, Grandma was reserved. If Will Geer, as Grandpa, gave the least sign of amorous intentions she would call him "an old fool" and swat him with a broom, and when she did on rare occasions smile, it was wonderful.

At the beginning was not the last time we were to

Ellen Corby

disagree. Ellen was well aware of the dangers of working with seven appealing child actors, each one of them a scoundrel without conscience when it came to stealing a scene. She also was aware that Will Geer knew every trick in the book to take attention away from the actor he would be playing a scene with. Richard Thomas had a conscience and a respect for the older actors in the series, but he was also aware that he not only had star billing, he *was* the star. All these things presented a challenge to Ellen. She solved it by rewriting the scripts.

Ellen had a genuine talent for writing and so in order to make sure that Grandma's presence was as prominent as possible she began taking a two-page scene in which Grandma did not have a great deal to do and expanding the scene to four pages in which Grandma dominated everything.

I was sympathetic to Ellen's predicament and let her get away with it for years. And then one day she went too far. She came into my office and laid the scene she had revised in front of me. She had taken a three-page scene and expanded it to ten pages. Grandma had all the good lines, all the good action, and even a couple of pretty good jokes.

I was not amused.

"Ellen," I said, "I'm not going to let you do this."

She looked at me and the wrath in her face built by the second.

"But . . ." she said.

"No buts . . ." I said firmly.

She turned and marched to the door. Making a measured and dramatic turn, as only an actress could do well and in fury, she looked back to me and said exactly what was on her mind.

"You son-of-a-bitch!" She made her exit and slammed the door behind her.

Ellen and I never stayed angry with each other for long, for in truth we loved and respected each other, and in no time we were back in our old routine.

One morning Ellen did not show up for work. This was cause for alarm. Ellen was never late. She never missed a day's work. If Ellen wasn't on the set at the appointed time, something was very wrong. Claylene Jones, the producer, went to Ellen's house and behind the curtained window saw a hand waving weakly. It was Ellen's. She had suffered a serious stroke.

The stroke left Ellen with severe speech and motor difficulties. Over time she learned to walk again, and with a cane could get from one place to another with only a small amount of difficulty. When we learned from her friend Stella that Ellen intended to return to work we were saddened. We knew it would be impossible.

We were wrong.

Ellen turned all of her energy to recovering her health. She worked with a speech therapist. She worked with a physical therapist, applying herself to that one single goal: to get back to her job.

With a great deal of misgiving, after her doctor's permission and approval, executive producers Rod Peterson and Claire Whitaker wrote a script especially tailored to Ellen's capabilities. It was called "Grandma Comes Home," and the story line was that Grandma comes home from the hospital after an illness, but is so pampered and protected that she feels old, useless, and no longer needed.

In the script Olivia asks Grandma why she is so

unhappy and Ellen is called upon to say the only two words she has in the show: "Need me."

In the filming of the show Ellen did well. Without speeches she simply pantomimed her part, and her ability as an actress came through. With the cameras rolling we all held our breath when that moment came for her to speak. It was difficult for everybody but especially for Ellen. Finally, the words came forth.

"Neeeeeeeedddddd mmeeeeeeee!"

It was a shattering moment. Ellen had provided us with a heartbreaking demonstration of human courage and strength. She had reclaimed her job and her life and she continued to act on the show as effectively, if not more so, until her final illness.

I went to see her in the hospital. It was early evening and the nurse directed me to Ellen's room. She was sleeping, a tiny little figure covered by a sheet.

Her window faced west and I thought I would not wake her, but simply sit and watch the setting sun and commune with the Ellen I had known and loved.

I detected a slight movement in the bedclothes so I went to her and leaned over. Her eyes were open and I said, "Ellen, it's Earl. Do you know me?"

With difficulty, she said, "Yessssssss."

"Do you know that I love you?" I asked.

Again she said, "Yessssssssss." I kissed her on the cheek and left.

A few days later Ellen was gone.

Michael Learned called to say that Ellen's ashes were to be placed in her crypt at Forest Lawn, and she asked if I would like to be there. I said I would.

When the day came I wondered what I could do for Ellen that would be appropriate. I thought of taking flowers, but my guess was that Ellen would hate flowers. And then I had an inspiration.

I spent an entire morning at the typewriter, and when I finished I had one of the best scenes I have ever written. Grandma had all the action, all the jokes, and all the good lines. She dominated the entire scene. I printed the scene, folded it, and stuck it in my coat jacket.

After the brief service at Forest Lawn I placed the folded scene at the foot of the column that contained Ellen's crypt. Stella asked what it was and I explained.

She said, "Well, you're not going to leave it there. It goes in with her ashes." And it was done.

Whenever and wherever Ellen wakes she will find the best scene of her career waiting for her. And she will be assured that I still love her.

THE GIFT OF CONCERN
Lillian Carter—Herself

Lillian Carter, mother of former President Carter, was convinced that I neglected and abused my own mother. And she spoke to me sharply!

It was winter, and I was in Virginia filming some location shots for a Walton special called *A Decade of the Waltons*. It was truly special because for the first time I was to going to introduce my mother and my real brothers and sisters to the television audience. We had filmed the actors in Hollywood ahead of time. The real person and the film of the actor who portrayed him or her would be matched up in the editing room when we returned to California.

I was away from my mother's house checking on a location we were going to use when the production assistant came running, all out of breath, and said, "The president's mother is over at your house!"

"President of what?" I asked. "Who are you talking about?"

"The president's mother, Miss Lillian Carter!"

President Carter and Lillian Carter

"What's she doing there?" I asked.

"She said she wanted to meet your mother."

I raced home and went into the living room. My mother and Mrs. Carter, both with blankets over their shoulders, were chatting away animatedly and they both looked up when I came skidding into the room. Mrs. Carter observed me with a look I could only interpret as hostile.

"This is my son Earl," said my mother matter of factly. "Earl, this is Mrs. Carter. She's Jimmy Carter's mother."

"How do you do?" I responded. She gave me a cool

look which I found puzzling. I resisted the temptation to ask what she might be doing in this part of the country. I found out later she had been politicking for her son, and when she heard that she was close to the "real" Walton's Mountain she had instructed her driver to take her to meet "the mother."

"Your mother and I are doing just fine," Miss Lillian answered, "but I want to speak to you when we're finished here. You wait outside."

After a while she came out on the porch where I had waited and she fixed me with an accusing stare.

I felt as if she had grabbed me by my lapels and was about to give me a good shaking.

"You work out in Hollywood, isn't that right?"

"Yes, ma'am," I answered.

"They pay you well?"

"Yes, ma'am."

"Then how come you can't get enough money together to give your mother a warm living room?"

She started walking toward the front gate and I trailed after her trying to explain that because of the filming all the doors were open so as to allow cables in and out. I also said quite honestly that my mother kept the rooms heated to near ninety degrees most of the time and that today was an exception.

I am not sure she heard a word I said. When we reached the front gate she observed that the latch that was supposed to keep the gate closed malfunctioned.

"And fix this gate," she ordered.

I promised I'd see to it promptly. She looked at me for a moment, and I wondered if she really knew who I was and if she had ever seen *The Waltons* or if the local politicos had simply brought her by for whatever political gain the visit might provide.

And then said, "What's that one with the mole like?"

I replied that Richard Thomas was a good friend.

"Appears to be a fine young man," she said.

"He's a wonderful person," I said. "He does a much better job of playing me than I do of being me."

"Appears to think well of his mother," she replied, then turned to the limo where her driver was holding the door open.

I smiled and waved as she was driven away, but she never looked back.

When I got back to my mother's freezing living room, I asked, "What did you and Mrs. Carter talk about?"

"Our sons," she answered.

THE GIFT OF GRACIOUSNESS

Minnie Pearl—Personality

In 1983 I created a television series for NBC called *Boone*. It was the story of Boone Sawyer, a young country singer who, in his sister's words, "wants to drive a purple Cadillac and live in a hotel." Actually, the character went a little deeper than that. Boone was born to sing. Without being Elvis, there was a lot of Elvis in Boone. His music flowed from the country he came from and from the folk and the folk music of the Tennessee hills, from the church music he had been raised on, and from his exposure to the blues and spirituals he had come to revere through his mentor, an elderly blind black man.

In addition to his own goals in life, Boone was pulled in two very different directions by his parents. His father wants his son to join him at his service station. There the father plans to teach his son to be an auto mechanic. His mother urges him to study for the ministry. Neither of these options is attractive to Boone.

A most talented and distinguished gentleman, Paul Wendkos, directed the pilot. The cast was a dream come true. An attractive young leading man who could sing like an angel, Tom Byrd, played Boone. His sidekick and buddy was an engaging young actor from Tennessee, Greg Webb. One of the most able and versatile actors of today, Barry Corbin, was the father, and the mother was the excellent Elizabeth Huddle. I was especially thrilled that Ronnie Claire Edwards, who was better known as Corabeth on *The Waltons*, came aboard and created another of her unforgettable characters.

It was decided that we would film the pilot in Nashville, the home of country music. It was a dream come true for me because I had grown up listening to the Grand Ole Opry, and I felt the prospect of actually filming in Nashville would lead to another hit show. Jane, too, was pleased at the prospect of a visit to Nashville because she had attended Ward-Belmont, a school known today as Harpeth Hall.

Nashville turned out to be an ideal location in every way. The people were hospitable and generous. One scene we needed to shoot on a horse farm. The owner of the farm we selected would not accept payment. When we convinced him that we had to have a contract, he agreed it would be all right if we paid him a dollar.

Another location called for a concert hall where

Courtesy of Country Music Hall of Fame® and Museum

Minnie Pearl

Boone is to audition for a job on the Grand Ole Opry. To our great delight the owners of the Ryman Auditorium allowed us to film there. It was the same stage where the original Grand Ole Opry had been broadcast from 1943 to 1974. It was built by a riverboat captain named Thomas G. Ryman and has been called the Mother Church of Country Music. It has perfect acoustics.

To add to the flavor and authenticity of the film, we

were also able to get permission to film a scene at a bar adjacent to the Ryman called Tootsie's Orchid Lounge, properly called Queen of the Honky-Tonks. The place defies description, but if you are ever in Nashville *go there*!

Filming on location means you spread a lot of Hollywood money around. That fact was not lost on the governor, who arranged a reception at the governor's mansion for our actors and crew.

One of his neighbors was the performer known as Minnie Pearl. Minnie was one of the country's best-known comediennes. In every appearance she wore the same straw hat with a $1.98 price tag dangling from it. The character was supposed to be a man-crazy spinster in the town of Grinder's Switch. Her entrance on stage was accompanied by her well-known holler: "Howdeeeeeee! I'm just so proud to be here!"

I did not know it at the time but Minnie's favorite television show was *The Waltons*. At the governor's reception I saw her enter the front door. I went over, introduced myself and said, "Minnie, I have loved you all my life, and I never expected to meet you."

"Honey," she said, "I feel the same way about you."

We spent a long time together that evening. She was keen to know everything about my series, and I could tell from her questions that she had seen just about every episode.

Minnie was far from the shrill backwoods citizen of

Grinder's Switch she portrayed. In real life she was a very cultivated woman from Centerville, Tennessee, who was well educated, had taught dancing, and toured the country with a legitimate theater company. During World War II she met and married Nashville pilot Henry Cannon, and as Sarah Cannon became a mainstay in Nashville society.

When Minnie met Jane and learned that Jane too had attended Harpeth Hall she insisted on taking Jane for a visit to the school and a tour of Nashville.

Later, after taking the tour, Jane told me that Minnie had shown the same friendly and open personality to everyone and been greeted warmly everywhere as "Mrs. Cannon."

Some years later I learned that she had suffered a stroke. I wrote to her from time to time telling her news about *The Waltons* as well as about Jane and me.

I never received a reply, but I never needed one. It had been reward enough for her to say: "Honey, I feel the same way about you."

THE GIFT OF ROYALTY

Jane Wyman—Actress

Miss Wyman belongs to that level of Hollywood society that can only be called regal. The period when she did her best work was the same time of such great names as Katharine Hepburn, Gary Cooper, Bette Davis, Clark Gable, and Ingrid Bergman. They were extraordinary people with such personal magnetism on screen that they were luminous. They were stars.

Miss Wyman was and is a star.

Even today when she is rarely seen in public she is a star. And she taught me what it was like to be a star.

I wrote a television pilot called *Falcon Crest* about a family that owned a vineyard in the Napa Valley. I based it loosely on an article in *Time* magazine about the emerging wine industry and several articles about wine dynasties in the Napa Valley.

Miss Wyman was our first choice when it came to casting the matriarch, Angela Giobertti. I met her for the first time at the Sacramento Airport a day or so before we were to start filming on location.

Jane Wyman

I had rented the longest, most impressive limo I could find. She smiled a greeting, stepped inside the limo, and after a few preliminary "get-acquainted words" she launched into a discussion of her character that was right on target and her remarks about the script were knowledgeable, informed, and useful.

I told her we had made arrangements for her to stay at one of the local country clubs. She said, "No, I want to stay where the crew stays." I rearranged her living accommodations so she stayed at the Holiday

Inn with the rest of us. It was a sound move, for it put her in touch with the technicians, drivers, make-up people, and costume people she would be working with. They liked her for being available. She knew what she was doing. Stars know what they are doing.

I needed a private conversation with the lady so I called her and said that we needed to have a talk and that I had made reservations at Jimmy's, one of the more up-scale restaurants in Beverly Hills.

"Good," she said. "They know me."

I added, "And I asked for a table in the back so we could talk without interruption."

"Call them back and tell them to give us my usual table," she said. "I never sit in the back of the room." Star talk. Hollywood royalty.

The series was fun and our cast was rich with great actors. Jane was without doubt the star, but we also had such fine actors as Susan Sullivan and Robert Foxworth, David Selby, Ana-Alicia, and Lorenzo Lamas, Margaret Ladd, Abby Dalton, and Chao-Li Chi.

Other excellent guest stars were attracted to the show. We were a hit, but they also came because Jane was our star and they knew certain standards would be set. Mel Ferrar became a running character, as did Caesar Romero. It became "the thing to do" for guest stars to join the cast. Gina Lollobrigiga came from Italy for a series of episodes. Kim Novak left her hideaway at Big Sur long enough to lend her enchanting presence.

One of the most controversial stars to join us was Lana Turner. When Jane learned that I had cast Lana she said, "I wish you had mentioned you were casting her."

"Why?" I said. "She'll be good for the ratings. What's wrong with casting her?"

"She's not a lady," Jane replied.

Jane was polite, but distant when Lana came aboard. At one point the CBS photographer asked if he could take a shot of the two of them together.

I explained to Jane what the photographer wanted and Jane said, "Bring her over."

Next I went to Lana and explained about the photographer wanting a shot of her with Jane.

"Bring her over," said Lana obligingly.

In the end, the photographer got his picture. He took it just as a scene between the two of them was ending and they were walking off the sound stage in chilly silence.

Lana provided an unforgettable moment in the filming. Most of the costumes were provided by our own costume department, but Lana had a dress she was fond of, and she insisted on wearing it for a particular scene. The gown was a spectacular piece of work, with hundreds of semi-precious stones woven into the fabric. It sparkled enough to light up dark places miles away, but because of the number of stones it was extremely heavy.

In filming there is a place called "the mark." It is usually a chalk mark on the floor where the actor is to stop when he or she comes into position for the scene being filmed.

Lana, in the heavy, sparkly gown made a stately entrance. It would have been an unforgettable piece of film, except for the fact that when she hit her mark Lana stopped but her dress continued moving.

In the end, my association with *Falcon Crest* became messy and disagreeable. I resigned after the first five years, but agreed to stay on as a consultant.

Strange things happened before I realized that I had been caught in one of Hollywood's most vicious games. Clearly, I, the creator of the series and the man who had guided it through five successful years, would still be of immeasurable help. Not so. The people I was supposed to consult with were never there for our appointments.

What was reported to the network was that *I* was the one who was never there, and in the end my lucrative consultancy was canceled.

I have been told that Miss Wyman did everything she could to keep me on the show as a consultant and for that I will always be grateful to her.

The series continued for three more years, but it became laughable. The storylines (and this takes some doing on a show of this kind) became absurd and in the end the audience drifted away.

It was not a worthy fate for Miss Wyman. She deserved better and it was difficult to see her trying to keep the series afloat when it was clear that it had fallen into incompetent hands.

I would have the opportunity to see her from time to time when she attended the traditional Christmas party at Harry and Patty Harris' house. Often she would be accompanied by her daughter, Maureen, who was an equally gracious lady. On these occasions, Jane would greet other guests cordially.

Some would often approach her like subjects being received by a queen, often waiting in line for a turn to chat. Even when not having seen some actor or member of one of her crews for years, Jane would remember every single name and would also ask about some relative or child or colleague.

Today Jane is retired and lives in Palm Springs.

My association with her was a highlight of my career, and if she reads this, I send my love and continuing respect. I know, but I won't tell, her age. I will reveal, however, that she is over forty, as regal as ever, and that she still has the best legs in Hollywood.

THE GIFT OF SOLACE

Isis Ringrose—Friend

In my books, movies, and television series I have portrayed my hometown as the repository of all those traditional American values that have sustained our
people throughout our history, and which are still celebrated in our culture today.

Yet the person in Schuyler who best epitomizes
those values, in my opinion, was not born anywhere
near Virginia, but in a place with the exotic name of
Ordzenikitzeabat!

Her name is Isis E. Ringrose, and Isis is a writer, a
musician, a humanitarian, and a psychic.

A psychic, by most definitions, is a man or woman
who can gain information in ways not explainable
within the framework of most scientific principals.

Unfortunately, the image many of us gain of a psychic is that of a gypsy with a bandana wrapped
around her head, peering out of the door of a store-
front in a seedy part of town. At the other end of the
spectrum are members of the American Association of

Professional Psychics who have been tested for ethics, professional standards, and proven psychic ability.

The advice of a psychic once even affected life at the White House. Nancy Reagan, understandably fearful following the assassination attempt on her husband, began consulting psychic Joan Quigley. Mrs. Reagan was said to change the president's schedule according to Quigley's advice.

Another indication of psychics coming into the mainstream of our daily lives is *Medium* on NBC, one of its most popular and innovative television series. The program is built around a housewife who can see and hear dead people. Using this gift, she helps solve crimes. The series was inspired by a real-life police consultant Allison Dubois.

Isis Ringrose's natal place of Ordzenikitzeabat is a village in the foothills of the Himalayan Mountains in what is now Russia. It is located at the edge of Tibet where Tibet meets with China and present-day Russia. The journey from the foothills of the Himalayas to the foothills of the Blue Ridge Mountains of Virginia is a stunning one, filled with danger, hardships and challenges, but driven and illuminated by one family's search for a secure, comfortable, and dignified way of life.

The details of that trek are dramatic and often harrowing. I will touch only on the highlights of it in this telling. Isis herself must relate the real story and she

Îsis Ringrose

will do so in her autobiography.

Until she was three years old Isis lived in the afore-mentioned Ordzenikitzeabat, a small village whose chief activity was herding sheep. It was a place of extreme weather, frighteningly frigid winters and summers so scorchingly hot that people would wrap wet cloth around their bodies for a brief cooling off and sometimes would sleep wrapped in wet sheets. The green valleys provided rich grazing pastures for the sheep. The surrounding mountains were so high and terrain so steep that guides would blindfold travelers along narrow mountain roads to keep them from realizing how treacherous were the narrow paths they traveled. Isis remembers generous, kindly, self-sufficient people of the area. Especially she recalls the image of native women washing clothes by pounding them on the smooth rocks in the bed of a river fed by hot mountain springs.

To go beyond the borders of the country was forbidden, but Isis's father was an industrious and frugal man who had accumulated some wealth. Anxious to provide a better life for his family, he paid corrupt border guides and smuggled his family out of the country.

Isis remembers the journey vividly. They made it by foot, horse cart, and finally by train on a journey reminiscent of the train ride to Siberia in the film *Dr. Zhivago*. On the windowless train car people were packed upright together with hardly space to breathe.

For a while the family settled in Poland. Isis's father, always looking for a better life for his family, attempted to smuggle them into Germany, but they were apprehended and sent back to Poland. Determined to reach a destination where they would be safe, Isis's father made Israel their goal. It was forbidden to take any property out of the country, so he had a cane devised with a hidden hollow chamber where he concealed enough currency to insure their safety until they reached a place where they might be welcome.

Hope appeared briefly when the ship they were aboard, loaded with people who had fled the only homes they had ever known, tried to go ashore in Venice, Italy, but they were refused permission to land. Isis ruefully remembers a visit to Venice many years later when as a tourist she stood on St. Mark's Square and looked out to the lagoon where she and her family, desperate for a toehold almost anywhere, had once been barred from entering.

Isis was seven and a half when the ship finally landed in Haifa. Even being sprayed with DDT did little to relieve their joy at finally reaching The Promised Land.

Israel was far from the modern country it is today. Refugees were herded into deserted British Army barracks. There were often fifty people to a room with cots to sleep on and an army blanket for warmth. And the occupants were from every imaginable country. During her travels Isis had already learned Russian, Polish, Yiddish, German, Arabic, and Romanish. Here she began learning French as well as Hebrew.

The family was moved next to a refugee camp called Pardes Hanah. Isis remembers the camp as being luxurious compared to their previous accommodations.

To her delight there was not one school, but two, a

secular school and a religious school. Isis was an eager student and managed to attend both.

Not knowing what grade she belonged in, the teachers placed her in the first grade. They quickly realized that she was much more qualified and began moving her up from one grade to another. She spent two weeks in each grade until her parents realized such promotions could prove harmful and put a stop to it.

School brought into even greater focus a strange gift she had been given. From her earliest days Isis was aware that there was some insight she had been given that was to be a burden as well as a blessing.

She sometimes knew that a thing was going to happen before it happened! Once when she was only a little girl, in another place and time, she made a prediction at school that came true. It was in a superstitious and ignorant community and she was stoned by the other children on the walk home from school. Even then Isis was proud of her gift and refused to run or allow the other children to intimidate her.

Equally frightening was the reaction of the adults when her classmates told them what Isis had done. They called her a witch and made the sign of Satan each time she passed. Isis knew she was different but did not fully recognize the difference for what it was at first. She knew only that a window would open for her that was not available to other children in her class, or knowledge that she logically would not have available would come into her consciousness. It took many years for her to come to know the name for this gift. She had psychic powers.

But now she was in Israel and at long last learning Hebrew. First she read and spoke the Old Hebrew, but a year and a half later she was speaking the New Hebrew. She loved reading the Bible and read it so constantly that she started speaking in Biblical jargon, "Would thou pass the milk?" "Hast thee done thou homework!"

When she was thirteen the family moved to Tel Aviv. They found lodging in a poor part of the city, but Isis remembers it with pleasure. Their quarters were on the second floor of the Shuk Hacarmel, an exotic street market where everything from watermelon to clothing, from herbs to spices could be purchased. Isis remembers what an exciting trip it was to go food shopping for her mother and to make her way through merchants singing about the freshness of their watermelon or the beauty of their fresh potatoes. The market is still there today, although it is considerably more upscale than when Isis and her family lived there.

When she was eighteen Isis was conscripted into the Israeli Army where she became assistant to an Intelligence officer. Given an opportunity to audition for the equivalent of the American USO, she did so and discovered a talent for performing, acting, and singing. For the remainder of her military service she went from base to base entertaining service men and women.

Her parents had already immigrated to the United States, and upon the close of her military duty she left Israel and joined her mother, father, and sister in New York City.

Here she met Tom Ringrose, the leader, or teacher as he is called, of a group of people who were forming a communal living association called "The Gathering." It was my great pleasure to know Tom Ringrose and to witness many of the gifts he brought to my hometown. He, like Isis, was a devoted and caring friend of my mother and became a meaningful part of our family.

The members of The Gathering are disciples of Edgar Cayce, who might be called the father of the psychic movement in this country. Edgar was a remarkable man who could look into the future and foretell with great accuracy events that were to come. He was an expert on the interpretation of dreams, spoke with authority about holistic medicine and near death experiences. Cayce founded the Association for Research and Enlightenment for the study of psychic phenomena, an organization still active today. Cayce died in 1945, but his work continues.

Tragedy was to strike "the Gathering" in 2005. Tom Ringrose, always subject to asthma attacks, suffered a fatal attack. He died in Isis's arms and is mourned by his followers from all over the world.

Today Isis still lives as a member of The Gathering. The members of the group are friends I have known for many years, for their home is in my hometown in the building that formerly held the company that owned and operated Schuyler Hospital. I feel a very special bond with the group inasmuch as three of my siblings and I were born in what was then the delivery room when it was a hospital.

The Gathering is best described in the words of its founder, Teacher Tom Ringrose:

> We are a spiritual group whose aim is a closer relationship with God as individuals and as a group. We came together in New York City in 1968 and began moving into ten acres in Virginia in 1975; at present we have fourteen members.
>
> We have our own system of economics, combining elements of income sharing as well as individual finances. We work for the refinement and uplifting of the quality of life as expressed in our spiritual practices, our creative endeavors (nursing, art, carpentry, design, carving, building, med-

icine, etc.), the enhancements of our
environment, our relationships with
each other, our economic systems and
the development of our menus and
cooking practices.

We pray and meditate together on
a daily basis, and our spiritual format
incorporates elements of the Old and
New Testament, as well as a wide
range of Eastern and contemporary
teachings.

We believe that the communal
style of living is the future and the key
to survival. It is the best format for development of the individual and the
evolution of civilization.

I have known Isis for many years and she never
fails to astonish me. I noted earlier that she is a writer,
a musician, a humanitarian, as well as a psychic.

She once allowed me to read part of a manuscript
she had written, a work in progress that documents
the life of the ancient Jews while in exile in Egypt. It
is an extraordinary document, filled with larger-than-
life Biblical characters who come vividly to life, with
images so magical that it was hard to envision their
being conceptualized, a dazzling combination of history, fiction, and gifted storytelling.

When I asked her about her writing she replied that she simply listens. She is careful to point out that this is not "automatic writing" but words that she received from another entity and that she records what she hears from another place and time.

From the amazing verisimilitude of her description of life for the Jews in ancient Egypt is easy to accept that it is told from a firsthand account. Isis is a Biblical scholar and as a description of this ability she cites Chronicles I, 28:19.

I have a tape of a piece of music Isis has composed. It is symphonic in nature and features several running themes which are delicate and memorable and unlike any other music I have ever heard. Again she received it by listening, and then having what she heard transcribed by a musician.

In 2006 Isis suffered a severe stroke which left her with some motor difficulty on her left side. Because of her strength and determination those of us who love her know that she will recover completely. Until her stroke Isis spent much of her time working for the good of the community. Many people in the area live on substandard incomes or are housebound. Isis made the rounds of bakeries, grocery stores and markets in nearby Charlottesville. There she collected food that is still edible, but that otherwise would go to waste and distributed it to needy people in the county. She plans to return to this work as soon as her health permits.

While I admire Isis for her talent as a writer, a musician and her dedication to helping people in need, she has given me an additional gift—the gift of solace and comfort in the face of great loss.

I have to admit that for most of my life I have been a cynic about people who claim to have psychic powers. Isis has generously shared discussions about the psychic world, and today I have become much less cynical and more of a believer.

There have been two events in my life which I cannot explain other than to label them psychic occurrences.

When Jane and I first moved to California we could not afford an office where I could write, so I set up a desk in the garage. I left the door open for ventilation, but I also enjoyed a passing parade of folks who would peer in and ask, "What are you doing?"

One of those who stopped by often, a local resident known as Peter the Hermit was a very old gentleman who dressed all in white and who occasionally rode by on a donkey. Home for Peter was a guesthouse on the property of an actor who lived nearby who provided Peter a place to live.

Peter once stopped by to say hello, looked at a photo of Sue Salter, who had been Jane's Maid of Honor at our wedding, and said, "I can tell you her birth date!" And he did!

A lucky guess? No way.

Peter made an even more stunning statement on another visit. When I told him I was putting the finishing touches on my new novel he said very casually, "Put the word *mountain* in the title and it will become a bestseller."

Spencer's Mountain hit the *New York Times* bestseller list a year later.

Another event in my life has been startlingly mysterious. The last few years of my brother James's life were especially sad and painful ones. Jim was the last of us to live in our old family home. As long as he lived there he would sit on the front porch and wave or answer back to the tourists who would call out "Hey, Jim-Bob!" While representing me Jim became unpopular with a small clique in my hometown. Toxic neighbors harassed him without cause and without justification. Heart attacks and emphysema took over his body and it was clear that he did not have long to live.

On the morning I was told that Jim had died I went to my car, which was in my garage and which had been locked all night. When I opened the door and was about to get into the driver's seat I noticed three small, shiny, glassy-looking objects. When I examined them I discovered what appeared to be three clear semioval plastic globes smaller than the end of one's little finger. They looked like tears that had solidified. I held them in my hand and I asked myself *Is*

this a message from Jim? Is he telling me that he is weeping?
I kept the little round ovals in the car until three days
later when they disappeared. If I had to supply an ex-
planation I would say that at long last Jim's tears were
gone and this was his way of telling me that the sad
days were over.

Isis has known my family for many years and
knows what they would do in almost any circum-
stance, even how one of us might conduct ourselves
after death. My father died in 1969. When my
mother died some years later Isis made the comforting statement:

"She is not alone. Your father was waiting for
her." Yes, I thought. My father would do that. Their
love was strong, and I had no doubt that shed of his
physical body there would still be a soul, a spirit, an
entity of some kind that would wait for my mother to
join him.

Jim and I had been particularly close. He had been
my "baby" brother, the last one of us to live in
Schuyler. Living in the house where we had all grown
up he kept it open, alive, and functioning. As long as
Jim lived in the house "home" still existed.

Jim died the very day I was scheduled to fly to Virginia to visit him. I had phoned him a few days ahead of
time and I did not want it to appear that I was coming
because I knew he was dying. I just said, "I have to be
back East and thought I would drop by and see you."

"You'd better," he replied.

Audrey was to tell me later that she felt it was merciful that I had not seen Jim toward the end because he was suffering so terribly, and he looked so bad that she wanted me to remember him in happier times.

Did he allow himself to go before I got there so as to spare me the anguish of seeing him suffer? I don't know, but the question comes to my mind.

Jim died in Audrey's arms. Reinforced by Isis's image of relatives waiting, I was able to believe that he went from Audrey's arms into the waiting arms of others who had loved him, and who had gone on before him, and I like to believe that one day they will also be waiting there for me.

For the gifts of solace and comfort in time of grief I am indebted to my friend Isis Ringrose, a writer, a musician, a humanitarian, and a psychic, who came to my village from half a world away.

THE GIFT OF LANGUAGE

Agripina Salvador—Friend

I have always wanted to speak Spanish. I suppose the first Spanish words I ever heard back there in the hills of Virginia were in songs I heard on the radio.

When I attended the University of Richmond I took a course in the language. The professor, Dr. Caylor, did his best to instill some respect for Spanish culture, but he concentrated on Madrid and Barcelona and Seville. I cannot remember any mention made of Mexico City, or Guadalajara, or Tijuana, or anything positive about a huge group of our neighbors, a Spanish-speaking people who live just over the other side of the Rio Grande River.

I first encountered "Spanish" when we moved from New York to Los Angeles in 1961. I had no car and it was frustrating to instruct a cab driver to take me to an address on La Cienega or Tujunga Boulevard. The words did not come readily to my back-country Blue Ridge countrified English. But gradually, as Jane and

Pina Salvador

I made ourselves at home here in Studio City and my ear became more accustomed to the language, I fell in love with it all over again. I wanted to speak it.

I wanted to learn the words to all those songs I heard on the radio, most of them having to do with declarations of love and references to their *corazons*. I have learned later on that as a people they are guided very much by what is happening in their *corazons*, and I am all for that.

Of all of the injustices we as a country have promoted to other countries, one of the most deplorable is the image we have projected of our neighbors to the

south as slothful individuals sleeping through their
siesta, their heads covered by a sombrero.

In truth, they are an industrious, hard-working people. People who should know better claim they take
jobs away from American workers. In truth, they take
jobs most Americans do not want or will not do such as
gardeners, busboys, short-order cooks, and laborers.

There is a delicacy about the Mexican people I
know, a refinement that expresses itself in a regard for
the other person. One Mexican friend of mine is so
courteous as to be courtly. His name is Nacho, and he
is the best tree trimmer in the world. To see him out
there on the limb of a tree is to see an artist at work.

I have even written a poem about him:

> Ignacio, the tree man
> Adores the senoras.
> He trims their
> Tree limbs carefully
> And casts them looks amorous.
> Up in the tree
> He leaps about
> Is Toreador for a day
> The ladies look up lovingly
> While his helpers shout
> Olé!

The opportunity to really learn Spanish came when

we first met Pina, who agreed to work for us as a housekeeper. She is a beautiful woman with soft brown skin and glistening black hair that she wears in a knot but must reach to her waist when it is loose. The initial impression of Pina is one of personal dignity mixed in with the most open friendliness. She has a lovely, wide round face and dark eyes, and is not truly Mexican but Indian. Pina is an extremely intelligent woman. She attacks every problem with logic and reason until the solution is found.

Spanish is the second language Pina had to learn. Her first language is an obscure pre-Columbian tongue spoken by the Zapotec Indians. It is a foreign language even to most Mexican people.

The Zapotec are a group of three hundred thousand people who live in the valleys and mountains of the state of Oaxaca. They are the descendants of an ancient civilization that flourished in a highly developed culture two thousand years ago. The Zapotecs are said to have built the ruins at Mitla, which they claim is the tomb of their ancestors.

Their early conception of creation was that they emerged from the earth, or that they turned from trees and jaguars into people. Another common belief among the ancients was that they were descended from supernatural beings who lived in the clouds, and that they returned there upon death.

Their descendants are an intelligent, progressive,

hard-working, proud people. They make good soldiers, outstanding leaders, and model citizens. Known worldwide as master weavers, they make rugs and wall hangings in intricate geometric designs and brilliant colors.

There is a large colony of people of Zapotec ancestry living in California today. Since the language is unique and some of those living here have not yet learned English, there is a lively demand for translators who know Spanish and Zapoteca as well as English.

Our friend Pina was born in the Zapotec village of Yohueche in Oaxaca, about forty miles from the city of Villa Alta. Agriculture is the main occupation in Yohueche, but the citizens also make a richly colored pottery, imaginative clay animal figures, beautiful weavings, and potent mescal.

When Pina was growing up, there was no electricity, no post office, and no running water. Candlelight supplied illumination and, as Pina laughingly recalls, the family car was a burro.

She learned Spanish in the local school in Yohueche. In order to help her family she left home when she was fourteen to take a job as a nanny with a family in Tijuana. From baby-sitting Pina graduated to cook and eventually traveled with the family to the United States on a tourist visa.

Pina fell in love with the country and was deter-

mined to return. She applied for citizenship and became a citizen in 1996—one of the proudest days in
her life. Pina takes her citizenship seriously. She not
only votes but she researches each candidate and issue
beforehand so her vote is an informed and deliberate
one.

Her husband, also of Indian heritage, is a chef at an
exclusive Los Angeles restaurant. Their daughter is in
medical school, and their two sons both have part-
time jobs and attend college part time.

Like many of my Latina friends, Pina has an artistic bent. Her flower arrangements are models of structure and color and harmony. When the children have
finished their education it is her ambition to open a
florist shop, and knowing the lady I have no doubt
that she will not just achieve her goal but excel at it.

When Pina first came to work at our house, I
would speak to her in my faltering Spanish. I confessed my love of the language and she generously
began coaching me in pronunciation. Later, Pina
would introduce a new word each time she came to
work. From single words we graduated to phrases
and finally to sentences.

As we progressed I became more fluent in conversation and was better able to communicate with the
many Mexican artisans who do work at our house,
from gardening to brick laying.

Pina is a tough teacher. She will have me repeat a

word until I have the pronunciation exactly right. I, on the other hand, will correct her pronunciation of English words.

We are a good team.

Gracias, Pina! *Usted es una buena professora!*

THE GIFT OF LOVE (AGAIN)

Caroline Spencer Hamner—Daughter

In May of 1956, in the maternity ward at Doctors' Hospital in New York City, Dr. Sevigney came out of the delivery room and announced, "You have a son!"

I did not think that life could ever again reward me with such an awesome moment. In those days the husband was banished from the maternity area of the hospital, but I had managed to see Jane as she was wheeled from the labor room to the delivery room. Her beautiful blonde hair fell to one side of the gurney, some terrible privacy of her body had been violated, she did not seem to see me, and I could tell that she was in great pain.

I resolved that we would never make love again. The price was too great. I could not bear to see her experience such pain. In spite of my declaration, two years later on September 3rd, Dr. Sevigney emerged from the same room and announced, "You have a daughter!"

And once again I was struck with awe. Shortly, I

was led to the viewing room and saw her! The stately beauty she is today was not all that apparent in those first few hours. Her little nose was smushed in, her face was red and splotchy, and she had very little hair.

Our friend, Sue Salter, took one look that first day and said diplomatically, "Well, Janie, she's a baby!"

But within days the nose took on the aristocratic shape it bears to this day, her skin turned from red to pink, and Jane had taped a little pink bow on our daughter's head. She was already becoming a great beauty.

Becoming the father of a son is one thing. Becoming the father of a daughter is another. You resolve to teach your son the workings of the internal combustion machine even though you don't know the slightest thing about how the internal combustion machine works. You become intoxicated on visions of a son's future accomplishments—the home run when the score is tied, the winning of the diving event, the ivy crown being presenting for high jumping at the Olympics.

It made no difference to my fevered mind that I could not swim, nor had I ever hit a home run or learned to high jump. I would learn. I would learn and I would impart to him all the practical, manly knowledge he would need in his life.

Different visions come to mind with the birth of a daughter. Perhaps it is because fathers are men and know that we are lustful, untrustworthy, and evil. We do not trust other men. We do not even trust little boys the same age as our daughters, because we know they will grow up to be just like us: Filled with uncontrollable lust, untrustworthy of pity, cesspools of evil.

We look to our daughters and start planning the construction of the tower where we will keep them safe. Only her mother and I will have the key and no male will enter unless he has been castrated several times!

But, alas, it is the way of the world that we cannot keep our daughters out of harm's way, and happily my obsessive need to be protective soon wore off and I allowed my daughter the freedom to grow.

There is a romance between father and daughter from the very beginning. Boys are hard and muscular and they bite. Girl children are soft and cuddly and learn early on how to wrap men around their little fingers.

Our son and our daughter spent their early "toddler" years in an apartment in Brooklyn Heights and later in a "garden" apartment at 44 West 12th Street in New York City. There was some competition between them for our love, but except for the rare occasions when they tried to kill each other their relationship was cordial. In 1961 we moved to Studio City, California.

The street we live on is called Amanda Drive, and

it was here that our children grew up. There were packs of children on the street in those days and they roamed about recklessly plundering and pillaging the neighborhood refrigerators, pools, treehouses and backyards. The street has a rural ambiance even though it is well within the boundaries of Studio City.

The street is pretty, a narrow, twisted country-like road that dead ends around the corner from our home. Frequently drivers find themselves lost, confused and frustrated. Some of them gun their motors to get the hell out of the puzzling cul de sac. Others slow down and will ask directions for getting back to one of the major crossroads.

In those days there were gangs of children on Amanda, exploring life, interacting with each other, finding their place in the group.

Caroline has always been a sensitive person. Once looking out across the valley to where the San Gabriel Mountains were shrouded in fog, she observed: "The mountains have little dreams on them."

When she was just a little girl Jane and I noticed something very admirable but at the same time alarming. When some driver would slow down and lean out of his or her conveyance in frustration, she would recognize the driver's distress and call, "Are you lost? Can I help you?"

She would then proceed to give precise directions to help the driver reach Laurel Canyon or Ventura

Boulevard or whatever street he was trying to find. Even though it was a more innocent world in those days and people were more trustworthy, Jane and I recognized her attempt to help other people could inadvertently lead to trouble. Trying not to alarm her we did our best to teach her to be cautious.

No matter the danger it was clear even from childhood that Caroline felt the need to reach out to people, to help those who were lost to find their way again.

After she graduated from Oakwood, Caroline continued her education at Claremont College in Pomona, a small town to the east of Los Angeles. She did well there, earned good grades, cultivated good friends and seemed quite happy until her junior year.

That year she took advantage of a year of study abroad that the college provided; she spent her studies in Rome. It was a wonderful experience that enriched her life for all time and changed her life in a significant way.

Shortly after she returned to Pomona she phoned one day and said, "After a year on the Via Veneto, I cannot live in this cow pasture."

She was quitting school!

Jane and I were opposed to her plan, tried to point out that she was making a mistake, but she persisted.

We played our trump card, smugly assuming we could force her to stay in school.

Caroline Spencer Hamner

"If you quit school you will have to find a job, a place to live, to support yourself," we threatened, feeling damn sure our side had won.

We were wrong. Caroline left school, found her own apartment, took a series of jobs and became totally self-sufficient.

Eventually Caroline went back to college and took her degree and went to work as a family therapist. Today she is married to a fine man, Pepe Mercado, a

computer expert whose weekend hobby is racing sail-
boats. They have a good life and enjoy gardening and
caring for a houseful of dogs and cats. Caroline still
works as a therapist and specializes in treating those
with alcohol and drug-related issues.

I see her now, just as she did when she was a little
girl, asking some distressed, confused, needy person,
"Are you lost? Can I help you?"

This is a desperate, lonely, and uncertain world we
live in. We seem to have lost our way, and all those
fine old customs like courtesy and gratitude and sac-
rifice and respect and kindness seem in short supply.
The world has become increasingly dangerous, at
least in the part where I live. Here in California we
shoot each other on freeways or pull over and stab
someone who has "cut us off." We invade people's
homes at night, tie them up and take their possessions
after giving them a good slap or two. Some of our
gang warfare spills over into residential streets, and
frequently takes the life of some innocent bystander.

We are cut off from each other socially, isolated by
economics and geography, frightened at the changes
that are taking place, susceptible to threats from all
sides. In our isolation and fear and distrust we become
dangerous to each other and ourselves.

And while all this is going on our leaders pontifi-
cate, posture, and give us "spin," when what we need
is truth and real leadership. We are given hypocrisy

and hype while the country is divided into two equally different ideologies, losing sight of the fact that it is still one country.

For all of the uncertainty in the world, here in this little corner of it, it comforts me that there is at least one person I know who reaches out to people who need help and is able to help them make their lives better.

And if they listen she can help them find their way home again. I know, too, that every action has a ripple effect, and I wonder what might happen if each of us threw aside our suspicions and prejudices and hatreds and our smug self-importance and called out to someone who seems to be in need, "Are you lost? Can I help you?"

Caroline still does that, and in so doing she makes this a better world for all of us.

ABOUT THE AUTHOR

EARL HAMNER is best known as the creator and producer of the Emmy Award-winning series *The Waltons* and *Falcon Crest*. The producer of many other televisions series and specials, he has also written for *The Twilight Zone* and *CBS Playhouse* and has penned many screenplays, including the award-winning *Charlotte's Web*. The author of eight best-selling books—including *Spencer's Mountain, The Homecoming, You Can't Get There from Here, Goodnight John-Boy*, and *The Avocado Drive Zoo*—he lives in Studio City, California.